Nikki Riggsbee

Bernese Mountain Dogs

Everything About Purchase, Care, Nutrition, Behavior, and Training

Filled with Full-color Photographs
Illustrations by Pam Tanzey

BARRON'S

CONTENTS

MEET THE BERNESE MOUNTAIN DOG

Born to utility, in service for centuries to the herdsmen and farmers of Switzerland, the Bernese Mountain Dog has found a place today as companion and member of the family.

Description

The Bernese Mountain Dog is a large, striking, tricolor dog, one of the most popular from Switzerland. The broad head, folded ears, dark eyes, and distinct markings contribute to the beautiful, friendly expression that reflects a calm but alert nature. Developed in the Swiss canton of Bern as a general purpose farm dog, the Berner has the deep, broad body, substantial bone, and combination of strength and agility that was well suited for many tasks on the farm. The same characteristics that made the Berner a valued farm hand in the past make her a treasured family companion today. In addition to their place in the family, Berners also serve today as assistance dogs, therapy dogs, and search and rescue dogs.

Snow, mountains, and hilly farmland are reminiscent of the landscape of Switzerland, the original home of the Bernese Mountain Dog.

Coat

The Berner's distinct coat is moderately long and either straight or wavy; curly coats are not preferred. It is a double coat, with the outer coat longer and the undercoat shorter and softer. Dirt tends to fall off a good healthy coat, so they are fairly easy to keep clean. The well-groomed coat doesn't usually tend to mat or tangle. It sheds throughout the year, however, and a major shedding of the undercoat occurs once or twice a year. Twice-weekly brushing should help keep the shedding under some degree of control.

Puppies begin with a thick, fuzzy, shorter coat. Older puppies and adolescents can go through a wavy or curly coat stage. The final adult coat should be straight or wavy with a healthy sheen. The Berner's coat does not require much trimming.

Color and Markings

The distinctive color pattern of black, rust, and white is one of the characteristics of the

The moderately long, black base coat and typical rust and white markings are characteristic of the Bernese Mountain Dog.

TIP

Berner Size

The Bernese is a large dog, though not too large to be agile. Adult males range from 25 to 27½ inches (63.5–68.5 cm), measured at the top of the shoulder, and from 90 to 130 pounds (41–59 kg). Adult females measure from 23 to 26 inches (58–66 cm) and usually weigh between 75 and 100 pounds (34–45 kg).

Bernese Mountain Dog. The base color on the body is black. Tan or rust markings are above each eye, on the cheeks, on the legs, on each side of the forechest, and underneath the tail. White appears on the muzzle, as a blaze on the skull, and on the chest, feet, and tail tip. The rust color usually separates the white from the black coat on the legs. The pattern of white on the forechest often looks like an inverted cross.

A great variety of face markings give each dog an individual and unique expression. Markings on the rest of the dog can vary greatly too. Some Berners have little if any white on the front feet; some have no white on the tip of the tail. Some have wide face blazes; others have narrow blazes. While symmetry of markings is desirable, this varies with each individual. Markings are important, but their contribution is to accentuate this eye-catching, handsome dog. They are important, but not more than the Berner's other characteristics. Breeders refer to this as "building the house first, then painting it."

The great varieties of markings add to the Berner's individuality and style.

History and Development

Bernese Mountain Dogs may belong to the Mastiff family of powerful and protective guardians. Perhaps they arrived when the Romans crossed the Alps, bringing their Molossus dogs with them from ancient Rome. However, skeletal remains of large-breed dogs have been found in Helvetia, the area now known as Switzerland, and these bones have been dated to a time long before the Roman Empire. So the Berner's connection to the Roman Molossus is primarily conjecture.

Early Records

People include their hunting and toy dogs in art and literature, but not working farm dogs, so there is no good record of the antecedents of the Bernese Mountain Dog. A 1651 painting by Dutch artist Paulus Potter includes a large tricolor dog similar to a Berner. Paintings in 1773 by Swiss painter Freudenberg illustrate farm scenes with large tricolored farm dogs.

Swiss Farm Dogs

General Swiss-type farm dogs probably existed from at least the fourteenth century. They likely had some uniformity since they were bred locally for functional purposes, uninfluenced by outsiders, but they were not purebred dogs as we know them today.

These farm dogs provided many services for their owners. They drove cattle to grazing fields, back home again, and then to market. They pulled carts of milk, sometimes alone or at other times accompanied by a young child from the family. They also protected the isolated farms from wandering beggars and unattached soldiers looking for handouts and more.

A reliable temperament was important for these tasks, including a reasonable reserve toward strangers. Size and strength were essential, as were intelligence, obedience, and self-confidence. The dogs were expected to stay around the farm and livestock as needed, and not go running off on a whim. Butchers and tradesmen used them as well, for driving cattle and pulling carts.

Bernese Mountain Dogs are descendants of the early Sennenhunds, who were the dogs of the Alpine herdsmen. These Sennenhunds did not have the consistent color and markings that we see in Berners today.

The Industrial Revolution reduced the need for farm dogs. As roads and transportation improved, dogs weren't used as much to pull carts. Other dogs such as the Swiss Saint Bernard and the imported German Shepherd Dog caught the Swiss public's fancy. By the mid-1800s, the local farm dogs became scarce.

Sennenhunds

The early farm dogs traditionally didn't have breed names as such. They were described by their color or markings, by the amount of white in their coats, by the region in Switzerland where they were found, or they were just called farm dogs or butcher dogs. Some of the Swiss farm dogs were eventually called Sennenhunds. Senn is a mountain herdsman, so the Sennenhund was the mountain herdsman's dog.

Durrbachlers

A large tricolor Swiss farm dog was found south of Bern in a town named Durrbach. These local dogs were called Durrbachs or Durrbachlers. A Burgdorf innkeeper named Franz Schertenlieb acquired one in 1890 and was so impressed with the breed that in 1892 he made an effort to round up the similar dogs in the area to preserve the breed. While they were similar, they varied in color and markings and the amount of white they had; some had a yellow or red base coat.

With Schertenlieb's enthusiasm for the breed and new European interest in dogs and exhibiting them, some people in Switzerland and other countries became interested in the Durrbachlers. In the early 1900s, Fritz Probst sought recognition of the breed from the Swiss Kennel Club. The Durrbachlers were the original Bernese Mountain Dogs.

Professor Albert Heim of Zurich, considered the father of the Bernese Mountain Dog, wrote extensively of the Durrbachler, helping to increase its popularity. In 1904 the breed was first exhibited at the Bern International Dog Show. Heim was instrumental in forming the first national breed club.

Heim campaigned to have the name of the Durrbachlers changed to Berner Sennenhund to be consistent with the names of other Swiss farm dogs that were being called Sennenhunds along with the name of the region where they developed. The national breed club finally went along with Heim's recommended name change.

A standard describing the breed was written to help make the dogs more uniform. The early dogs varied a great deal. Heim encouraged selective breeding to correct such faults as split noses, tails curled over the back, double dew-claws on the rear feet, yellow eyes, and curly coats. Breeders were encouraged to have their dogs conform to the color and markings as described in the standard.

Early Berner Sennenhund breeders and owners wanted the functional characteristics to be paramount, believing that those were the virtues that made the breed useful and popular. The dogs should be able and willing to protect the farm, its residents, and the livestock. They should have reliable and stable temperaments and should be willing to stay on the farm and not run off.

Newfoundland Cross

While the Berner's popularity was growing in the twentieth century, it was held back somewhat due to its shy and reserved temperament. In 1948 a breeding took place in Switzerland between a Bernese female and a black Newfoundland, a breed known for its sweet, gentle temperament. The breeding is presumed to be an accident, albeit a fortuitous one for Bernese Mountain Dogs.

The resulting litter improved the Berner temperament and gave the puppies wider, deeper chests and more lustrous, longer, and straighter black coats. But the puppies were mostly black like Newfs, not tricolor marked like Berners. A female from this litter was bred to a male Bernese Mountain Dog, producing puppies that retained the good qualities of the first cross and regained the Berner color pattern on most of the puppies. A female from the second litter was also bred to another Berner, producing a litter of good quality correctly marked Bernese Mountain Dogs. One of the males in this third

Historically, Berners were used as general purpose farm dogs. Their large, hardy frames made them ideal for pulling carts to market, a task they can still perform today.

TIP

What's in a Name

Bernese Mountain Dogs have different names in different countries:

Switzerland	Berner Sennenhund or Durrbach dog
Germany	Berner Sennenhund
England	Swiss or Bernese Mountain Dog
France	Bouvier Bernois
United States	Bernese Mountain Dog

The Illustrated Bernese Mountain Dog

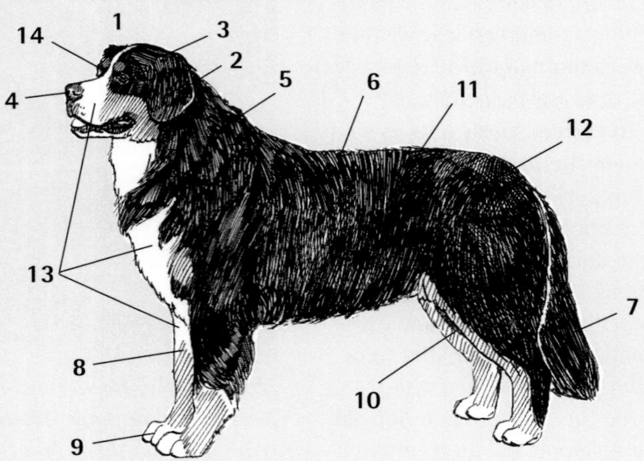

1. Striking tricolored large dog, longer in body than tall, sturdy bone, full body.
2. Ears medium sized, set high, triangular.
3. Skull flat on top and broad.
4. Nose always black.
5. Neck strong, muscular, and of medium length.
6. Topline level, back broad and firm.
7. Bushy tail.
8. Legs straight and strong.
9. Feet round and compact with well-arched toes.
10. Thighs are broad, strong, and muscular.
11. Coat thick, moderately long, and slightly wavy or straight.
12. Ground color jet black.
13. Markings rich rust and clear white.
14. Rust over each eye, on the cheeks reaching to at least the corner of the mouth, on each side of the chest, on all four legs, and under the tail. A white blaze and muzzle band, a white marking on the chest typically forming an inverted cross, and white on the tip of the tail.

litter subsequently sired 51 champions and is in the pedigrees of most of the Bernese Mountain Dogs today.

This cross with the Newfoundland improved the Berner's temperament while retaining Berner type in color, markings, shape, and size, and it was accomplished in just three generations. Since then, Berners have bred true without the Newfoundland reappearing in the litters.

In the United States

The first Bernese Mountain Dog came to the United States in 1926, imported by Isaac Schiess. The American Kennel Club (AKC) didn't recognize the breed until 1937, however. The owner of the first AKC-registered Bernese was Glen Shadow of Louisiana. The first two he imported were named Fridy and Felix. They are credited with saving Shadow's life when he was attacked by a 10-point buck, which was subsequently killed and dressed out at 160 pounds (72.5 kg).

For more than ten years, Shadow was the only owner of AKC-registered Bernese Mountain Dogs. Registration and breeding increased in the mid-1950s. Several Bernese fanciers lived on the West Coast, and in 1967 a Bernese Mountain Dog breed club was formed in California. This club became the basis for the Bernese Mountain Dog Club of America, the breed's parent club, which was incorporated in 1972. Soon after recognition by the AKC, the club held the breed's first national specialty show in 1976.

The Berner-Newfoundland cross contributed to today's Berners' good temperament and long coat.

Related Breeds

There are four Sennenhunds—Swiss mountain dogs. All have similar coloration, with a black base coat, and rust and white markings. Because of their similarities, it is assumed that they came from similar origins and developed in fairly isolated areas in the Swiss Alps.

✔ The Bernese Mountain Dog is the only one with a long coat, which it had prior to the tryst with the Newfoundland. It is the second largest of the Swiss mountain dogs, at approximately 25 to 27½ inches (63.5–68.5 cm) and around 115 pounds (52 kg).

✔ The largest and probably the oldest Sennenhund is the Greater Swiss Mountain Dog, also called the Grosser Schweizer Sennenhund. It weighs about 125 pounds (57 kg) and is an inch or so taller than the Berner. Like the Bernese, the Swissie is AKC registered. It was developed near Burgdorf and primarily used as a draft and drover dog.

✔ The Appenzeller Mountain Dog or Appenzeller Sennenhund is smaller, at 18 to 22 inches (51–56 cm), 50 to 70 pounds (22–32 kg), than the Bernese. It has a curled tail and a short coat and often has more white than the other

Top row: Greater Swiss Mountain Dog (left) and Appenzeller (right). Bottom row: Bernese Mountain Dog (left) and Entlebucher (right).

Swiss mountain dogs. It is not AKC recognized. It is named for the canton of Appenzel in northeast Switzerland where it was developed. With speed and agility, it was used to herd and guard livestock.

✔ The Entlebucher, also called Entlebucher Sennenhund or Entlebucher Mountain Dog, is the smallest of the four, under 20 inches (51 cm) and 55 to 60 pounds (25–27 kg), and hails from the cantons of Entlebuch and Lucerne. It has a short coat. It may have a natural bobtail, a docked tail (if permitted and desired), or a now more frequently seen natural undocked tail. It functions as a shepherd's dog, a watch dog, and a drover.

Personality and Temperament

A Bernese Mountain Dog is good-natured, easygoing, self-confident, and alert. She can be a good watchdog, a trait inherited from her farm guardian ancestors in Switzerland, and is protective without being aggressive. She may remain watchful and aloof with strangers. Once she gets to know people, she usually welcomes them with each visit. She may announce the arrival of company, but most Berners are not gratuitous barkers. She may yodel on occasion, probably reminiscent of her Swiss heritage.

She is an intelligent and biddable dog, eager to please, but with a mind of her own. While easily trained, she thinks for herself and may figure out her own ways of doing things.

People Dogs

Berners are people dogs; they want to be where their family is, preferably in the same room, right next to them is ideal. Berner owners' list the breed's devotion and loyalty as among its cherished traits. The puppies and dogs need to be introduced regularly to many different people as part of their socialization. If isolated from people, they can become shy. They are devoted to their families; smart owners will develop the bond based on the great love the dogs have for their people.

Intelligent

The Berner is a smart dog; the smart owner will develop and cultivate that intelligence. If she is taught how to learn, especially at a young age, she can learn a great deal. Because she is and

TIP

Burner Bump

The Berner's interest in being close to their people is illustrated occasionally by the "Berner bump" to get attention or by nuzzling your hand or arm to remind you to pet them. They will lean on people—the doggy equivalent of a hug—and are happy to be touching their owners.

will be large, training must begin at an early age, hopefully even before the puppy comes home with you. The Berner puppy, and adult, too, is sensitive and doesn't respond well to the jerk and yank method of training. With this large dog, force will be less effective than rewards.

When reaching adolescence, many dogs, including Berners, will test their boundaries. These are big teenagers, so you may need to remind them of their limits and lessons. The dog is strong enough to pull a cart, and she can pull you down the street if you haven't leash-trained her.

Space and Exercise

Adult Bernese Mountain Dogs need moderate exercise; youngsters need more to expend their youthful energy. Homes in the country, including farms, are fine for Bernese, but the suburbs are too. Some Berners do well in apartments if they have the opportunity to exercise regularly. One is even reported living happily on a good-sized boat.

This is not a "speed demon" dog or one that needs to gallop much of the day. A relaxed trot suits her just fine. She enjoys joining the family for walks or visits to the park; car rides are also fun. But not in hot weather, please. Even with her heavy coat, the Berner is not exclusively a cold-weather dog. Yes, she probably enjoys winter best. But many Bernese Mountain Dogs live in warmer climates, provided that they have access to shade when outdoors, cool water, and air conditioning when needed inside, and exercise primarily in the cool of early morning or later evening.

The same characteristics that historically made the Berner a successful farm dog make her a great companion and family pet today.

Many people think a large, coated dog would be most comfortable outside, but they would be wrong—unless the Berner's family is outside, too. Bernese Mountain Dogs want and need to live where their families are, which is inside in

TIP

Berner Chuckle

Many Berner owners report that their dogs have a sense of humor. If you laugh at her antics, she's bound to do it again to tickle your fancy and get a reaction.

Teaching your Berner to stay *will help you to pose your dog and get great photographs.*

the house. In the house, the adult Berner has a relatively low level of activity. Puppies, of course, will sometimes be rowdy. Berners will adapt to the activity level of their people, for their first love is to be with their family.

Children and Other Pets

Bernese Mountain Dogs get on well with children and are tolerant of their behavior. If the children get to be too rambunctious, the dogs will just leave and go elsewhere.

The historic farm dog got on well with other farm animals and livestock. Most of today's Berners should get along with other household animals too.

Would You and a Bernese Mountain Dog Be Right for Each Other?

No breed is right for everyone, no matter how wonderful it is. You have several things to consider before you decide to include a Berner in your family.

Health

All breeds have some health conditions that may occur more frequently than in other dogs. This doesn't necessarily mean that most dogs of that breed will have the problem, but it is something the owners need to be aware of and recognize.

One health issue for Berners is cancer, specifically histiocytosis (see the chapter on health for a complete description). If a Bernese does not get cancer, she may live to 10 to 12 years, but the incidence of cancer reduces the average life span to 7 to 8 years.

Like other large dogs, Bernese may have some bone abnormalities. Elbow dysplasia is found, as is hip dysplasia. Ask your breeder if the puppies' parents and their relatives have been tested and found clear of these conditions. Remember that even cleared parents cannot guarantee that the offspring won't have the abnormal joint formation.

Hair

The moderately long tricolor coat is the crowning glory that contributes to the beauty of the Bernese Mountain Dog. It also contributes to hair that has been shed throughout your home. Brushing regularly will help, but there will still be hair. You can decorate in black, rust, and white, so the hair doesn't show as much. But, if you are a fastidious homemaker offended by some dog hair on the furniture, on the floor, under the bed, and elsewhere, you might want to consider another breed.

The lush coat is ideally suited to cold weather, of course. But if you live in a temperate climate or if you just have warm summers, you will need to keep your Berner inside in air conditioning, with exercise in the cooler times of the day.

Accommodations

Berners need room for exercise and a place to relieve themselves. A fenced yard is preferred for both. It doesn't need to be acreage, although that would be fine, but it must be securely fenced. Keep her on a leash when she is outside of your yard. She may stay close and usually come when called, but dogs can get distracted or momentarily run "to a different drummer." Don't bet her life expecting her to be perfectly obedient.

Size

Berners are big dogs. She may look like a cuddly teddy bear, but she is so much more. She will go through a rowdy puppy stage followed by a testing adolescence. Bernese mature slowly but do not live particularly long. The Swiss say, "three years a young dog, three years a good dog, and three years an old dog." Are you willing to train and teach and put up with your youngster until she blossoms into a sensible adult?

Time and Expense

Do you have time for this dog? Are you at home enough or is a great deal of time spent away from home? If you don't have adequate time at home with your Berner and cannot include her in your leisure activities, this might not be the right breed for you, if any is.

Can you afford this dog? The initial purchase price is just the beginning. Can you afford the quality food and veterinary care she will need in her life? No dog should ever lack for care because her owner cannot afford it.

Enjoying Your Berner

There is so much to enjoy about a Bernese Mountain Dog. She is stately and beautiful. She is easygoing and gets along well with people and other animals. She is affectionate, quiet, and loyal. She loves being with her family. She is intelligent and intuitive. Stories abound of Berners as companions, being considered the best dog the owners ever had.

Finally, check with all the members of the household. Are they all enthusiastic about adding this handsomely huggable big dog to the family? If so, you are ready to begin your search for a breeder and a puppy.

FINDING A BERNESE MOUNTAIN DOG

You've decided that a Bernese Mountain Dog would be the right breed to join your family. But where to get one, and how to find one?

Reputable Breeders

Your best chance to get a good-quality puppy is to find a reputable breeder. His puppies are most likely to have more of the physical and mental characteristics you expect and want from a typical Bernese Mountain Dog. His puppies are most likely to be healthy and have a good temperament.

Reputable breeders' primary purpose in breeding dogs is to continuously improve the breed, to have each generation be better than the preceding one. They breed dogs for themselves to include in their breeding programs. They can't keep all the puppies—the others in the litter are sold to people who want a Bernese to show and to people who want a pet. Reputable breeders breed dogs as a hobby, not as a money-making venture, so they are also called hobby breeders.

Deciding to bring a Berner into your life is a milestone for you, your family, and for the dog.

They are usually members of their breed's parent clubs. In the United States, this is the Bernese Mountain Dog Club of America (BMDCA); many other countries also have a national club for the breed. The parent club has a written standard for the breed that describes the perfect Bernese Mountain Dog. Reputable breeders try with each litter to produce dogs that conform as closely as possible to this standard.

Breeders evaluate their own dogs and take them to dog shows to get a more objective evaluation and to compare them with other breeders' dogs. At dog shows, AKC judges compare the Bernese Mountain Dogs entered and award championship points to one male and one female if they think the dogs are of high

When visiting a breeder, make a point to meet the whole family of dogs. The puppies will resemble the rest of the family both physically and mentally.

enough quality. Serious breeders compete to earn championships on their dogs, as confirmation that their dogs are good enough to be bred.

Reputable breeders are experts and resources for puppy buyers for the life of the dog. They are available to answer questions and offer suggestions and are your source for breed and dog information. They are also safety nets for their puppies. If a buyer cannot keep one of the breeder's dogs for any reason, the serious breeder will take the dog back and find it a new home.

Where Not to Get Puppies

Conversely, the place not to get a puppy is from anyone who is not a reputable breeder. Among these are commercial or high-volume breeders. They are money-making enterprises and less concerned with the quality or the future of their puppies. Their dogs are poorer quality and more likely to have problems later in life. They seldom sell their puppies directly to buyers who visit their premises; rather, they wholesale them or sell through a Web site. Commercially bred puppies are often more expensive than those from responsible breeders. High-volume breeders are sometimes called puppy mills since they are in the business of churning out large numbers of puppies for sale.

Backyard breeders are also not good sources for a quality Berner. They aren't as big as commercial breeders, but their goal also isn't the

Reputable breeders invest a great deal in their dogs and puppies and are very selective about the homes to which their dogs go.

improvement of the breed. Usually, their dogs are not of breeding quality. These breeders are making extra money. They are seldom experts in the breed and don't stand behind their dogs. Backyard breeders often sell their puppies through newspaper ads and now are using Internet ads and Web sites as well.

How to Tell Which Is Which

✔ Reputable breeders show their dogs, so most of their dogs will be champions. Look at the pedigree of a litter you are considering. One or both parents should be AKC champions, two or more of the grandparents should be champions, and at least half of the great-grandparents should be champions. Breeders who advertise "champion lines" may be breeding dogs that have just a few champions three or more generations back, but the dogs they are breeding are not champion-quality dogs. Some breeders with poorer-quality dogs may show their dogs occasionally, but they are seldom good enough to earn championships.

✔ Reputable breeders register their dogs with the American Kennel Club (AKC) in the United States or with the equivalent registry in other countries. They usually are members of their breed's parent club, such as the Bernese Mountain Dog Club of America, and of their regional Bernese club if one is available. They often are members of a local all-breed kennel club, too. Ask where the breeders register their dogs. Ask what dog clubs they belong to.

✔ Reputable breeders do health tests on their breeding stock. They are breeding for themselves, and they want healthy puppies too. They select the best Berners they can for breeding to further their goal of improving the breed. They select based on the dogs' correct physical traits, good temperament, and good health. Ask the breeder what health tests are done on the dogs.

Be wary if sellers tell you that their puppies come from imported stock that does not have the health problems of American dogs. Further questioning may reveal that the seller is a puppy broker who buys from puppy mills in

Visit breeders and meet their dogs; the dogs should be friendly, healthy, and well cared for.

Eastern Europe and Russia then resells them in the United States for an extravagant profit. Foreign-born Berners have the same types of health issues as American-bred Berners.

Responsible breeders are selective about who will get one of their puppies. They want to make sure each puppy will be well cared for during its whole life, and they want to be certain that you get the puppy that is best for you and your family. Even though they are willing to take the puppy back, they would rather the puppy be in a responsible, loving, lifelong

TIP

OFA: Orthopedic Foundation for Animals

You can see if a litter's parents have certain health clearances. If you have a dog's registered name, you can look him up on OFA's Web site, *www.offa.org*, and see if that dog has been evaluated for hip and elbow dysplasia and other conditions that reputable breeders check prior to breeding.

You can also access Berner-Garde, a foundation established by the BMDCA. It contains health information on individual dogs collected over the years from Berner owners. The Web address is *www.bernergarde.org.*

home. If the breeder does not ask a lot of questions about you, the dogs you've had, what you want in a dog, and how you will care for the dog, find another breeder.

Visit the Breeders

Visit each breeder from whom you are considering getting a puppy. Get to know him and his dog family in person if at all possible. The puppies will resemble his other dogs, both physically and mentally, so you are looking for a dog family that you like. The dogs should look healthy and well cared for. They should be friendly, although remember that Berners may have an initial reserve when they meet new people. Notice where and how the dogs are kept. Ideally, they should be in the house with their family.

Ask the breeders about their dogs and about Bernese Mountain Dogs as a breed. They should be very knowledgeable and be able to answer your questions. Good breeders welcome questions and will take the time to answer them. Ask about problems in the breed; breeders who have been breeding for some time will have encountered some. Breeders who claim to have encountered no problems either haven't been breeding very long or are not being candid.

You are really looking for a Bernese breeder rather than a puppy. Once you find the right breeder, one whose dogs you like, who is knowledgeable and honest, get on the list for a puppy from one of his litters.

Dog Clubs

Bernese Mountain Dog Club of America

The Bernese Mountain Dog Club of America (BMDCA) is the parent club and is responsible for the breed. It has a written standard describing the perfect Bernese that serious breeders should try to produce. The purpose of the club is to preserve and protect the breed and to promote understanding and appreciation of it. Its members are dedicated to Berners and support the club's purposes; they subscribe to a written code of conduct related to owning, showing, and breeding Berners.

The BMDCA has a Web site at *www.bmdca.org* that is full of helpful information about Bernese. Look at *Tips on Buying a Bernese Mountain Dog* in the *BMD Info Series* link for more suggestions on good breeders and on breeders to avoid. The site lists regional Bernese Mountain Dog clubs in the United States and the events scheduled by both the parent club and the regional clubs.

TIP

AKC Limited Registration

Limited registration is a type of AKC registration intended for dogs that will not be bred. Dogs with limited registration cannot enter conformation dog shows, and if they are bred, their puppies cannot be registered with AKC. They can, however, enter any other AKC event or competition for which they are eligible.

Under the *Puppies* link is information about finding a breeder and a puppy. A unique feature in this section is the *Breed Profiler.* You can select among several statements about what you want in a dog and descriptions of your home and family. The profiler will identify those places where you fit well with a Berner, and those areas that may be issues for you with this breed.

The American Kennel Club

Founded in 1884, the AKC is the oldest purebred dog registry in the United States. It maintains the registry, sanctions dog events held by affiliated clubs, and promotes responsible dog ownership. The AKC is a club of clubs, and those clubs are all over the country. AKC is the only not-for-profit dog registry in the United States.

Responsible Berner breeders in this country register their dogs with the AKC. Since the AKC requires breeders to maintain records to insure the integrity of the registry and has suspended breeders for inadequately caring for or maintaining their dogs, some breeders, especially commercial ones, have created their own "registries" so that puppy buyers can get "papers" with their dogs. Make sure that the breeders you are considering register their dogs with the AKC or with the equivalent primary registry in other countries, such as the Canadian Kennel Club, The Kennel Club (England), and the Bernese Mountain Dog Club of Switzerland.

Serious Berner breeders compete with their dogs at AKC events to earn titles on their dogs, including that of Champion. Note that other smaller event-giving organizations in the United States offer awards to participating dogs. The title of Champion from these non-AKC events is usually much easier to get, and dogs of lesser quality can earn this award. Make sure that the families of Bernese you are looking at

Confirm that you are dealing with a responsible, reputable breeder before losing your heart to an adorable puppy.

If you walk with your dog off-lead, make absolutely sure that you are far from traffic as well as from other people or dogs who might not welcome your Berner.

are AKC champions, or for imported dogs, that they have championships from significant award-giving organizations in other countries.

The AKC has a Web site, *www.akc.org*, that is full of useful information for any dog lover. You can also find lists of AKC activities around the country. If you click on *Events*, you can learn about the different kinds of events you are interested in, including Conformation (which are dog shows), Agility, Obedience, Rally, and Canine Good Citizen.

Dog Shows

Reputable Bernese Mountain Dog breeders show their dogs, so a dog show is a good place to find Berner owners and breeders. You can find shows in your area using the AKC's Web site. You can also find Berner specialty shows on the BMDCA site.

Dog shows run all day. Find out ahead of time whether there are any Berners entered, and if so, what time they are scheduled to show, before heading to the show.

Superintendents

Most all-breed shows are put on by superintendents who are engaged by the show-giving clubs. The superintendents will have the judging schedules on their Web sites for each of their shows about a week prior to the show date. From the schedule, you can see how many

This day, this dog was selected as the best Bernese Mountain Dog at the dog show. After they take photographs, you can ask to meet the dog and his people.

Bernese Mountain Dogs are entered and the time and ring where they will be shown.

To find the superintendent, from the AKC event list, click on the show you are interested in to get more details. This will include the name of the superintendent organization and its phone number. Additional superintendent contact information, including Web site and e-mail address, are also on the AKC's Web site. Click on *Events*, then click on *Conformation*, then click on *Superintendents*. You will see a list of superintendents licensed by the AKC. Find the one putting on the show you are interested in, and go to their Web site. Find the target show again on the superintendent's Web site to find the judging schedule, the number of Berners entered, and the time they will be shown.

At the Show

Get to the show at least a half-hour before Berners are scheduled to be shown. Wear comfortable clothes, especially comfortable shoes. Many shows do not provide chairs, so you might bring a small folding chair so you can sit when you want to.

When you find the Berner ring, you will see some people with their dogs. Introduce yourself and ask if they have time to talk. If they are getting ready to go in the ring, they might request that you visit after they have shown their dog. Meet as many Berner people as you can. You can ask them about the breed, whether they breed themselves, or where they got their dogs. Have pencil and paper handy so you can note names and contact data on Berner breeders and owners.

Best of all, you can meet the dogs themselves. Always ask first before petting a dog. Some are carefully groomed to go in the ring and aren't available for petting until they are finished showing.

Why You Should Care About Breeders and Pedigrees

Finding a breeder, interviewing him, being interviewed, and maybe going to a show is a lot of work. You just want a pet. Why should you care about reputable breeders and champion pedigrees?

You want them because you will be spending a lot of money on this dog and his care; you should get the quality pet you are paying for. This dog will be part of your family for years. You want him to be healthy and have a good temperament. You want access to reliable help and information that only a reputable breeder will provide. You will have this dog longer than you will have your computer or your car. Do

Puppies will be at least eight weeks old before going to their new homes. Some breeders keep puppies until they are ten or twelve weeks old before placing them.

your homework ahead of time to help insure that it will be a good experience all around.

Show or Pet?

At eight to twelve weeks, the breeder will begin to determine which puppies he considers as having show potential and which can be placed as pets. Show-potential puppies are those he considers most likely to earn their championship; the others in the litter can be sold as pets. In fact, all the puppies will be family companions. The difference is that the show potential puppies may have show careers as well.

Show Potential: The criteria the breeder is using to decide on show potential seldom have anything to do with the puppy's value as a pet. He may consider the size and position of the ears, eye color, and tail and tail carriage. He will look at body height and outline, coat color and pattern.

If you think you might want a show dog, discuss with the breeder what this involves. Show-potential puppies may cost more. They need to be kept intact—altered dogs cannot compete in dog shows. If you want to include this dog activity in your life, your breeder will help you select a suitable puppy and will be your mentor in showing your Berner.

Pet Quality: If you want a pet puppy, your breeder will probably sell the puppy with AKC limited registration. Many responsible breeders also require that pet puppies be spayed and neutered. Some will hold the registration papers or include themselves as the puppy's co-owners until they have confirmation that the dog has been altered. Make sure you see the registration papers or get a photocopy to have the AKC numbers of the sire and dam. Some disreputable breeders promise AKC registration papers that are never delivered.

Male or Female?

Male or female is usually a matter of personal preference, for both make wonderful pets. One of the biggest differences with Berners is that the males are several inches taller, heavier, stronger, and will eat somewhat more, especially as adolescents. Female dogs are often easier to house-train. When females urinate, one time empties their bladders. Males, on the other hand, may need to urinate two or more times to be empty. An intact male may mark his territory and may wander in search of love, although neutering usually avoids both of these issues. Intact females will shed heavily each time they come into season.

Puppy or Adult?

Most buyers want a young puppy. They are incredibly cute—as huggable as a stuffed toy. Because they are more in demand, young puppies usually cost more than older puppies or adults. People feel they can raise the puppy to be the dog they want and not inherit problems. On average, a puppy will have more years with your family than an adult.

The downside to getting an eight-week-old puppy is that he will need to be trained in everything.

- ✔ He will need to be house-trained.
- ✔ He will need to be civilized and socialized.
- ✔ He will need to learn not to put his mouth and teeth on the furniture, plants, electric cords, cats, and people.
- ✔ He will be high energy.
- ✔ While he will sleep a lot, when awake, he will run, jump, and play and can be a challenge to keep up with.

Puppies are a lot of work. Plus, you won't actually know what the puppy will be like as an adult. His personality has yet to completely develop, although the nurturing environment and socialization you provide can help him be all that he can be.

With an adult, you know what you are getting physically and mentally fairly quickly. They are usually trained to some degree, may already have sensible house manners, and may already know some useful commands such as "*Sit*" and

This eight-week-old puppy is already standing like a show dog.

"*Down.*" Their energy has moderated. They can keep up with you easily, but they are often content just to hang out and keep you company. When you meet them, you can learn early if they are outgoing or introverted, if they are athletic or a couch potato, if they have been raised with and like children, cats, or other dogs. If you don't have the time or energy to train a puppy, consider getting an adult.

Note: Breeders often have too many dogs; it is an occupational hazard. They may have kept a puppy that didn't turn out to be the show prospect they hoped for. They may have used one for breeding that didn't produce well or have taken a dog back that the original buyer could no longer keep. They could be looking for good "forever" homes for each of these.

Rescue

Another source of adult dogs is rescue. "Rescue" is the term used for the activity of, and people involved in, helping find new homes for dogs that have lost theirs. There are many reasons why a Berner might lose his home. Bad things can happen to good people: health problems, divorce, job loss, having to move. Some of these events cause families to give up their dog.

Unfortunately, some people consider pets disposable and give up a dog for which they no longer have time or that they find inconvenient. They may have bought a Berner on a whim. They may be unable to handle a large dog and haven't trained it. They may find the continuous shedding more than they can cope with. The problem is the previous owner, not the dog. With a little effort, an unlucky Berner can get very lucky and be a super pet in a new home.

Your New Puppy

You and your breeder have chosen each other. The litter has been born. You'll get your puppy soon.

Many people envision a pile of appealing puppies that they get to select from. In many cases, responsible breeders are involved in the selection of your puppy, whether it is pet- or show-potential. Some puppies may be reserved for other homes. You may want only male or female, which limits the number further. From your description of what you want and your family's home, the breeder may be in the best position to select the puppy whose temperament and personality are best suited for you. If you have been selected to get a puppy from a reputable breeder of a quality litter, you can consider that the puppy has been especially chosen for you.

A BERNESE MOUNTAIN DOG JOINS YOUR FAMILY

You need to prepare before bringing your Bernese Mountain Dog home. There are supplies to buy and things to do to get ready.

What to Get Before Your Berner Arrives

Food and Bowls

Buy some dog food just before she arrives. It is best to continue the same diet that she had at her breeder's home to avoid tummy upsets. She may not eat well initially, but she will after she is acclimated to her new home. Stainless steel bowls for food and water are easy to clean and won't break, chip, or crack as plastic, glass, or ceramic can.

Collars and Leads

People often buy industrial strength collars and leads for big dogs, but heavy-duty equipment isn't necessary. A 6 foot (1.8 m) single thickness lead is strong enough and easier to hold. Some folks like retractable leads, which have obvious advantages. But they are harder to hold, and if you accidentally let go, the plastic case will bounce along behind your running dog, as if it were chasing her. It is very frightening, and a panicked dog can run to exhaustion or into traffic.

Some people admire the longer hair on the Berner's ears as characteristic to the breed, while others trim it for a neater look.

There are many different styles of collars. She'll outgrow several sizes between puppy and adulthood. A single-thickness buckle collar works as does a quick-clip adjustable collar. Rolled leather or nylon collars can be easier on your Berner's coat. The slip-style collar can be used for training, but should never be left on the dog. Check weekly to see if the collar has become snug, and loosen it or get a larger size as needed.

Some owners like to put identification tags on collars to help recover the dog if she gets

A rolled or narrow nylon collar will wear your Berner's coat less. If there is no chance of escape, you can leave her collar off at home.

lost. Dogs should also be microchipped, which helps identify them, too. Other owners use collars only when taking the dog out on a lead and don't leave them on their dogs. With Berners, the collar can rub the coat. Further, collars have been involved in many accidents where dogs have been hurt or worse, either when the collar got caught on something or when two dogs were playing.

Toys

What's a homecoming without toys? Make sure they are sized for a large dog and don't have pieces that can be chewed off and swallowed. Berner puppies explore the world with their mouths, and they chew, both for entertainment and curiosity and because they are teething.

Sterilized bones, which may be flavored, have hollow centers into which you can put peanut butter or cheese spread that your puppy will enjoy licking out. Large knucklebones are good, but take them away when pieces are small enough to be swallowed or choked on. Rawhide, pigs' ears, hooves, and such are not good choices, for they are not digestible and can be swallowed. Emergency stomach surgery may be required to remove numerous pieces of undigested rawhide.

You can buy toys, but with a little imagination, you can find some around your house:

- An orange or an apple is a flavored ball.
- A carrot can be carried and chewed and is quite digestible.
- An empty plastic soft drink bottle or milk jug is fun to carry around and chase when they bounce erratically.

Don't give your puppy something you

Toys are fun and stimulate the senses. They also provide chewing opportunities and distract your Berner from playing with your toys.

Get a crate big enough to accommodate your Berner when she is an adult, with enough room for her to stand, turn around, and lie down comfortably.

wouldn't want her to chew in another circumstance, though, for she cannot tell the difference between the old shoe, for instance, and your new ones. These discovered toys can be discarded when the puppy has chewed them too much or when she is no longer interested.

Crate

Most breeders strongly recommend having a crate for their puppies. Think of a crate as a home-within-your-home for your Berner—it is her bed, a safe place of her own. It functions like a crib and playpen do for a baby, where you can keep an eye on your puppy, but where she cannot get into trouble. It is also a great boon to housetraining, for she won't want to mess her bed. Get one sized for an adult Berner, at least 28 inches (71 cm) high, 40 inches (102 cm) long, and 26 inches (66 cm) wide. This size will accommodate most Berners, though a really big male will need a bigger one. While crates come in plastic, many owners prefer metal because they last longer, are easy to clean, and collapse to a smaller size for storage. Inside a metal crate, your Berner can easily look out and see what is going on.

Grooming Products

Consult your breeder for grooming products and tools he recommends that you get to keep your Berner clean and beautiful. The short list should include

- shampoo formulated for dogs
- a large pin brush
- a tool for nail trimming
- a greyhound comb with metal teeth, good for getting burrs out of the coat and combing the soft hair behind the ears
- an ear cleaning liquid or rubbing alcohol with cotton balls to clean ears and get rid of wax buildup.

Get your puppy accustomed to gentle grooming within days of her homecoming. It should be a pleasant time for both of you

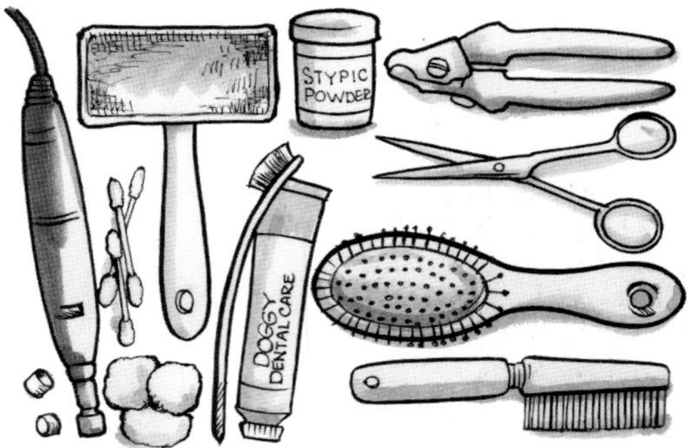

Grooming tools include a metal comb, pin brush, scissors, nail clipper or grinder, styptic powder, slicker brush, and dental and ear cleaning products.

TIP

Puppy Color

Your puppy will have a fluffy puppy coat with her own personal markings. As she grows, the white areas tend to get smaller, and the rust areas tend to get larger. So the adult marking may vary somewhat from what you see in your puppy.

A towel carrying the smells of her mother and littermates can calm your puppy during the trip home and through the initial days at her new home.

(see the Grooming section of the chapter *Caring for Your Berner*).

What to Get from Your Breeder

Registration Form

There are many things to get from your breeder when you pick up your puppy. He should provide the form to apply to register the puppy with the American Kennel Club. Make sure it is an AKC registration or the equivalent primary dog registry in countries other than the United States. Some breeders may have already registered their puppies. In this case, you will need the registration certificate to transfer the puppy to you as the new owner. Other breeders hold the registration applications until pet puppies have been spayed or neutered. In this case, you should see the registration application and record your puppy's future AKC number as well as the sire's and dam's registered names and numbers, all of which are on the form.

Sales Agreement

You should get a sales agreement or contract stating the terms of sale of the puppy. It should identify the breeder, you as the new owner, the registered names and numbers of the sire and dam, and the litter number or registration number of the puppy. It may specify how the puppy will be kept, the option to return her to the breeder if you no longer want her or can't care

There are over 20 regional breed clubs located in various parts of the United States. These clubs sponsor a variety of social and educational activities for Berner fanciers.

for her, and anything else the breeder considers important. You should have reviewed this document as part of your decision to get the puppy.

Health Information

Your breeder should provide health information for you and your veterinarian. It should include dates and details about when the puppies were born and worming medications and

TIP

Kennel Clubs in Other Countries

Australia—Australian National Kennel Council
Canada—Canadian Kennel Club
England—The Kennel Club
Germany—Verband für das Deutsche Hundewesen
Mexico—Federación Canófila Mexicana
Switzerland—Société Cynologique Suisse

inoculations administered. It can include the name and contact information of the veterinarian who saw the puppies. Some areas require that a veterinarian-signed health certificate be provided, too.

List of Food

Your breeder should list the food and amount the puppy has been eating plus her feeding schedule. He can tell you the grooming that has been done with the puppy and what he recommends. If you are traveling any distance, he may give you some food to last until you get home. You might also get some water that the puppy has been accustomed to drinking, so that her drinking water can be changed gradually.

TIP

Drink Enroute

If your Berner puppy is traveling in a crate, freeze some water in the plastic cup that comes with the crate to give her something to lick during the trip that won't spill.

Note: Arrange with the breeder to get a towel or something similar that has been with the litter for several days. It won't be pristine, but it will "smell like home" to the puppy and will comfort her during the transition. It is her security blanket that she can have with her in her crate during her days of getting used to her new home.

Traveling to Your Home

How your Bernese Mountain Dog puppy travels to your home depends on how far away she is coming from and your preferences. Schedule her arrival at a calm time when one or more family member can be home full time with her to ease her transition.

Car: One option is to travel by car, which can be a long or short trip. If the trip is short and you have another person with you, one can

Berners begin as cute, cuddly, teddy-bear-like puppies and then grow to be big, strong dogs. Before getting that cuddly puppy, be sure you are prepared for the big, strong dog she will soon become.

If you have hardwood or tile floors, provide soft cushions and beds for your Berner to lie on in order to reduce trauma to her bones.

drive and the other can hold the puppy. If it is a long trip or you don't have a companion with you, having her in a crate in your vehicle will keep her safe and comfortable—a towel from her home will add to her comfort. If the trip is long, schedule potty stops every hour or two.

Plane: Another option is for her to travel by plane. You will need an airline-approved crate to transport her. Shredded newspapers or incontinence pads in the bottom of the crate will keep her drier. Try for a nonstop flight if at all possible. An early morning flight in summer is cooler, and a midday flight is warmer in winter. Flights later in the day are more likely to be postponed, canceled, or have mechanical problems than earlier ones, so earlier is better to avoid those problems.

Your Berner Is Home!

When your Berner arrives at your home, take her to the place you want her to use to relieve herself. Let her wander around and sniff. If she hasn't gone in some time, she will eventually relieve herself. Praise her calmly while she is going or when she is just finished, perhaps giving her a little treat as a reward.

Stay with her as she explores your yard and house. Show her where the water bowl is kept. Introduce her to the family, making sure that no one overwhelms her. Let her make the overtures and discourage people from hovering over her. Encourage children to be calm, not run around, or make loud noises that may frighten the puppy, and supervise so that they treat her gently.

Two Berners are more than twice the fun. Your adult Berner can help teach your new puppy the house rules, the place to potty, and where the toys are kept.

Other Pets

Introduce her to other pets gradually in the house. You can let them sniff her in her crate. Monitor their behavior to avoid problems; don't just assume they will all get along. Make certain that they are friends before letting them outside together. Remember that the other pets were there first; give them priority so they won't resent the newcomer. Pet them first, give them treats first, let them go through the door first. The puppy will naturally respect their higher rank, and their relationship will be more harmonious if you respect the higher rank of the senior pets, too.

Crate and Bedding

It is a big day for her, and she will tire easily. Put your puppy in her crate with soft bedding for a nap. Give her the smells-like-home towel to make her more secure. When she wakes, she'll need to go out immediately to relieve herself.

Spend a lot of time with your puppy during her first days with her new family. Learn her ways, and let her learn the ways, sounds, and smells of your home. She will be learning, so this is also the time to begin gentle puppy training.

Initial Lessons

The whole world is new to a puppy, and your Berner is learning all the time. It is an ideal time to guide her to behaviors you want. Dogs are creatures of habit. It is up to you to make sure she develops habits that you consider good, and avoid those you don't want. Remember to be consistent, and she will learn more quickly how her new world works.

Crate Training

Crate training is accustoming the dog to relax in a crate. Your breeder may have had a crate available for the puppies, so she may already be comfortable in one. Dogs are den animals and will naturally find a corner or safe place. The crate can be that place. It should be big enough for an adult Berner. Put a mat or something soft inside for her to lie on, in addition to her towel. Add some toys and some chew bones. The crate is her bed and her haven. It can also be her dining room if you feed her in the crate.

Crates allow you to avoid problems by keeping her from forming bad habits. Baby puppies will spend more time in their crates, being out when

CHECKLIST

Berner-Proofing Your Home

1. Decide on the part of your home your Berner will have initial access to.
2. Get down on the floor and look at your home from your puppy's point of view. Identify anything that could be a danger to the puppy.
   - ✔ Wires and cords should be kept as much out of the way as possible.
   - ✔ Cleaning products and medicines are poisonous and must be stored in cabinets she cannot open.
   - ✔ Toxic plants must be placed where the dog cannot reach them.
3. Keep your kitchen garbage pail in a cupboard or closet, or get one with a lid to keep the temptation away from your puppy.
4. Chocolate is tasty, but it can make your dog sick, so keep it out of reach, too.
5. Puppies explore the world with their mouths and race around like toddlers. Avoid problems by moving breakable or chewable items from the area your puppy will be exploring.
6. Look outside, too. The yard your puppy will use should be securely fenced.
   - ✔ Check that there are no gaps that a curious puppy can get through or under.
   - ✔ Gates should close securely. When your Berner gets older, she may learn how to open gate latches, and you may need to lock the gate. Clips like those on the end of leads can effectively secure most chain link gates.
7. Plants outside may be poisonous, too, and should be removed to outside the puppy's yard. Dogs can play havoc with fragile plants in a landscaped yard. If this is your situation, you can go outside with her to keep her out of the garden.

the owners can play and pay attention to them. Little by little, as they mature and learn, they earn more freedom. The crate is still there, as a bed and a haven, though, even for an adult dog.

House-training

Crates are a boon for house-training, for your Berner puppy doesn't want to soil her bed. She will need to go when she wakes up, before or after meals, and during play. In her crate, she will fuss when nature calls, and you must get her outside immediately—within seconds, not minutes. It is a good idea to place the crate next to a door to her yard. Out of her crate, she will sniff the ground a few seconds before going. It is up to you to notice her signals and get her to the place you want her to use.

You can help house-training by giving her food and water on a schedule. What goes in on time comes out on time. Fix the times for her three daily meals at the same times every day, including weekends. Give her water when she gets her food plus two other times at specific hours during the day.

Recall

After house-training, the next priority pet owners want is for their dog to come when called. Dogs are pack animals that want to follow their leader—you. It is up to you to make sure that it is a positive experience for the dog to come to you.

✔ Get down to puppy level and call her in a happy excited voice.

✔ When she comes, pet her and praise her and give her a tiny treat.

✔ Reinforce this behavior by carrying treats with you and periodically calling the dog to you during the day, praising, petting, and treating her each time.

✔ Start by calling her when she is close to you, and progress to calling when she is a little further away. Set her up to succeed, making it totally wonderful to come to you.

Conversely, never, ever call her to you to do anything she considers unpleasant, such as getting a pill, a bath, or her toenails clipped. If you need her for something she won't like, go get her. Even when she has done something wrong, if she comes to you, always praise her; never punish her. If you punish her, you are teaching her *not* to come.

Bite Inhibition

Puppies explore their worlds with their mouths. They play with the littermates with their mouths; they tell each other in no uncertain terms when someone bites too hard. Our skin is more delicate than theirs, so they must learn from us to inhibit their bite reflex, to not put their mouths on people at all.

When your puppy puts her mouth on you or bites your clothing or your hair, put your hand on her muzzle and give it a small shake, and say "*No!*" or "*Ow!*" Repeat this as often as necessary. Have the rest of the family do the same.

Jumping

Having a dog jump on you can be very annoying, and a big dog can knock down a child or an elderly person, so it is incumbent on you to teach your Berner not to jump up. Fortunately, it is easy if you start with the puppy. When your Berner jumps on you, grab her paws, one in each hand, and hold her standing on her hind legs. Just hold her paws; don't talk to her. She'll pull her legs to get away, but keep holding. She may try to bite at your hands; move your hands out of reach, but still hold onto her paws. Hold her in that upright position for maybe a full 30 seconds or more. Then let her go and ignore her.

If she jumps again, grab her paws again, and repeat the "lesson." If she is reasonably bright, after two or three lessons, she may still jump. But she won't jump close enough to you to grab her paws. No sir! You aren't going to trick her again.

Chewing

Puppies chew. They chew because they are teething, examining something new, or are bored (see suggestions under "Toys," page 30). Don't give her access to things that you don't want her to chew. Crate her when you cannot watch her until she has learned what to chew and what not to chew. This will help keep her from developing bad habits.

Lead Training

To begin lead training, have your Berner wear a collar until she gets used to it. Then attach the lead, and follow where she wants to walk.

Children can practice reading to their Berner, who is always interested in a good story.

When she stops, position yourself at her right side and facing the same way. When she walks again, go with her. If she balks and pulls, wait until she stops fussing, then continue the walk. When she walks nicely, praise her and give her a treat.

When she is accustomed to a lead, she may pull. Pulling back is no solution, and may encourage her to pull more. Remember that Berners are draft dogs; pulling is a job they were bred for. There are two ways to reduce or eliminate pulling.

1. The first is easy. When she pulls, stop. When she looks back and there is slack in the lead, continue with the walk. When she pulls again, stop again. She will learn that the walk continues only when she doesn't pull.

2. The second method requires you to do a bit more—to change direction. When the lead is beginning to tighten with her pulling, turn sharply right or left or turn around and go in the opposite direction. Your Berner will be startled and thrown off balance, but she'll recover and come along. When she pulls again, change direction again. You've invented a new game where she must pay attention to you and where you are going or she'll miss the turns. She can't pull and keep an eye on you at the same time.

CARING FOR YOUR BERNER

You have found your well-bred puppy and brought him home. The dog he will become will be greatly influenced by the care you provide. It is incumbent upon you to provide quality "nurture" to continue the good job of "nature" done by your breeder.

Food and Feeding

The number and variety of available dog foods and canine diets are enough to boggle the mind, or at least be confusing. There are commercial foods from big and small companies in different forms, as well as homemade cooked and raw diets.

Commercial Dog Food

Commercial foods come in canned, semimoist, and dry varieties. The canned foods are the most palatable and also contain a high percentage of water. Semimoist foods are also tasty, but contain a lot of sugar and dyes to make them look meaty.

High-quality dry food provides the best choice of nutrition for your money among the commercial foods; many dogs like it dry or with water added. If your Berner is a picky eater, you can add some extras to make it more enticing. A bit of canned food, a sprinkle of Parmesan cheese, or a dribble of butter can entice a poor eater to consume more. Be careful, though, for adding goodies may turn him into a picky eater, willing to eat dog food only when the extras are included.

A mature male Berner is a large, handsome, powerful dog.

Your breeder and veterinarian can recommend high-quality dog food brands. It is usually a good choice to use well-known name brands. The larger companies have more resources for research and development and for quality control than the smaller "designer foods" or less expensive brand companies do. Larger companies are also more likely to get federal inspection of ingredients and processes, while smaller companies can fly below government radar.

Consult with your breeder and veterinarian about quality foods or diets you are consider-

Feed your Berner puppy large-breed puppy food. Regular puppy food is too enriched for large breeds and may result in bone problems.

ing. Do your homework, and look at your dog: If he is thriving and healthy, you can have confidence in his diet.

Amounts

Your breeder should tell you how much food and how often your Berner is eating when you get him. Puppies usually eat three or even four meals per day. The amount will depend on the puppy's age when you get him, perhaps 1 to 1½ cups per meal.

As he grows, add a bit more food to each meal. Note that dogs do not necessarily grow evenly, but rather in spurts with plateaus in between. Feel him through his coat to make sure he's not too thin or too chubby. At around five to six months, he will lose interest in the third meal. You can then feed him the same total daily amount split into two meals. It is best to continue with two meals a day for the rest of his life. He will be healthier and more comfortable to be neither starving nor stuffed. All dogs don't necessarily eat the same amount at each meal. Some like more in the morning, while others like more for dinner.

Males, being bigger, will tend to eat more than females at the same age. Active adolescents between 12 to 18 months will eat more than adults. As with people, the amount to keep your Berner healthy and fit will vary with the individual and his size, metabolism, and activity level.

Senior citizens need fewer calories than puppies and active adults, so feed them a food geared to seniors. Keep your older dog in good weight, for being fat will shorten his life. He needs good-quality protein even more now to keep his body fit. His digestive system is less efficient than it was when he was younger, so the quality of protein is more important than ever.

Homemade Diets

One of the trendy homemade diets is composed of raw foods with a significant amount of raw meat and bones. Usually vegetables and grains are added for balance.

These raw diets have not been scientifically tested to confirm that they provide the balanced nutrition your dog needs. Large breeds such as Bernese Mountain Dogs have an extra

Active older puppies and adolescents will eat more than adult dogs eat. Berners, like most dogs, will need more food when it is cold than in warm weather.

need for properly balanced foods while they are growing. Diets without nutrients in the ratios that rapidly growing puppies and teens need can lead to bone problems.

One of the arguments often used to promote a raw diet is that it is natural and is what dogs eat in the wild. But our dogs have been domesticated for thousands of years; they are not wild animals. Further, in the wild, animals don't live past their adult prime. As soon as they aren't faster than another predator, they become someone else's dinner. We hope for a long, healthy life for our dogs, and good, balanced food helps achieve that.

If you want to provide home-cooked meals for your dog, consult with your veterinarian for correctly balanced recipes.

Supplements

Probably the best advice regarding supplements for your dogs is simply "Don't" unless recommended by your veterinarian. A high-quality brand-name dog food targeted for your Berner's age and activity has what he needs. Adding supplements can unbalance his diet. Some believe that vitamin C is beneficial; since it is water soluble, it is unlikely to do harm, and any extra is passed in his urine.

TIP

Weight by Age

2 months	16–20 pounds (7.25–9 kg)
3 months	31–35 pounds (14–16 kg)
6 months	55–65 pounds (25–29 kg)
1 year	75–90 pounds (34–41 kg)
2 years	95–105 pounds (43–47.6 kg)

A puppy from a big litter may initially weigh a bit less than a puppy from a smaller litter. But later his genetics and care will determine his size. From two months until seven months, Berners will gain about 10 pounds (4.5 kg) per month, after which they will gain less quickly. Females will be lighter than the males.

The supplement most likely to cause problems for your growing Berner is calcium. Too much or too little calcium or calcium not precisely balanced with phosphorous can lead to various skeletal disorders and diseases.

Consult your breeder and veterinarian before giving supplements to review the types and amounts you are considering.

Treats

Treats are tasty; they are rewards for good behaviors and helpful training tools.

✔ Select your Berner's treats so that they contribute to his health.

✔ Read the ingredient label before selecting one.

✔ Don't give so many treats that your Berner is getting an equivalent of an extra meal's worth of goodies each day.

✔ Break treats into small pieces so you can offer them often without giving too much.

If you want to give a lot of treats, reduce the size of his meals.

Water

Water is critical to your Berner's good health. You might give a puppy water at regularly scheduled times to aid house-training: with each meal plus another two times during the day, but not within a couple of hours of bedtime. Make sure the water is fresh by changing it at least daily and washing the water bowl regularly. Dogs can pick up coccidia or giardia from stagnant water and get severe diarrhea.

Grooming

Start grooming your Berner as a young puppy, shortly after he joins your family. Make it a gentle part of your quality time together. One goal in grooming is hygiene, keeping him clean and sweet-smelling and welcome in your home. Another is to maintain him as a handsome representative of his breed, for he may be the only Bernese Mountain Dog that many people get to meet.

Brushing

Characteristic of your Berner is his striking tricolored medium-length coat. Brushing will help keep this coat beautiful and help keep his shedding under control. The more you brush, the less hair you will find shed all over your home!

Brush your Berner three times weekly or more when he is shedding.

✔ Begin at the tail and work forward.

✔ With each leg, start at the foot and work upwards.

When the coat is shedding, a rake can speed the process of removing dead hair.

✔ Using a large pin brush, brush his coat in sections, lifting the coat in front of and above the portion you are working on to insure you brush all the coat to the skin.

✔ Remember to brush the inside of each leg and the underside of his body.

Mats: A slicker brush, with shorter tines that are closer together than a pin brush, is useful for breaking up mats. Watch for mats behind the ears, inside the ear leather, and under his front legs where they meet his body. The coat on the ears may be a different texture than that on the body and tends to mat more often.

Shedding: If he is shedding, the dead hair can be removed with a rake, a grooming tool with short, moderately spaced tines used to remove loose hair from thick undercoats as well as to help remove mats and tangles. In colder climates, coated dogs shed twice a year; in warmer areas, Berners will shed year-round. Intact females will also shed immediately before or after being in season. Finish your brushing session by combing the coat with a large steel comb to make certain there are no tangles remaining. A greyhound comb is helpful for removing burrs and combing the hair on and behind the ears. Comb through the coat around the anus to remove any bits of fecal matter.

Feel him all over: During your brushing, feel your Berner all over. Check for any bumps, lumps, or abrasions. Your veterinarian must check out any lump or bump as soon as you can schedule an appointment. Check his weight so you can adjust his diet if he is too heavy or thin. Look for fleas—hard to find on a black dog. Part the coat and look at the skin level. Look for ticks, too, which tend to hide in armpits, and in and behind ears, although they can attach anywhere. The sooner you find a problem, the sooner you can attend to it.

Trimming

The Bernese Mountain Dog is a natural breed, but a bit of trimming can be done for the dog to be tidy and safe.

Trim the long hair that grows past the pads on the bottom of the feet.

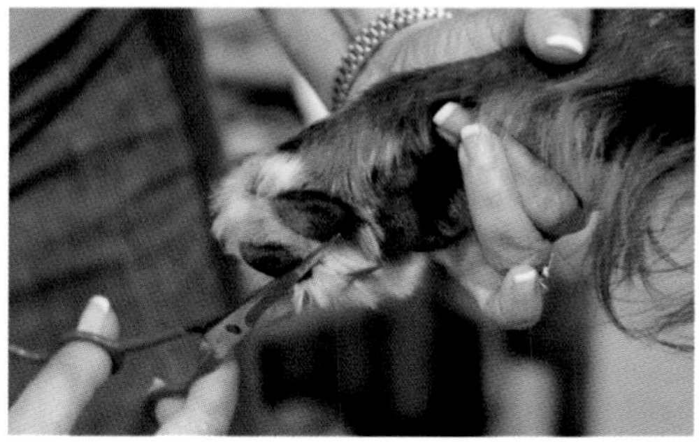

Clean both the inside of the ear and the inside of the earflap with a moistened cotton ball.

Trim long hair around the foot, especially the hair that grows between the pads. If left there, it can cause the dog to slip on slick surfaces. In cold weather, it can get wet and freeze.

Long, stringy hair and curly hair grows on the ears. If you like the look, keep it. Some people trim the long or curly hair on the ears with thinning shears.

Bathing

How often you bathe your Berner is up to you—how dirty he gets and how particular you are. Some bathe their dogs a few times a year; others prefer once a week. Choose whatever works for you.

- Brush your dog thoroughly before wetting him to remove any mats; otherwise, they will be harder to remove later.
- Put cotton balls in his ears to keep water from the ear canal.
- Use a good-quality protein shampoo formulated for dogs. Protein shampoos strengthen the coat and help avoid breaking and split ends. Consider a protein coat conditioner, too.

You may let your Berner air-dry provided he won't get chilled. Many people use a blow-dryer made for dogs to dry their dogs more quickly, especially in cooler weather. It doesn't get as hot as hair dryers people use, which get too hot to be safely used on dogs. Use a towel to get dripping water from the coat. Then put your dog in a crate and focus the canine blow-dryer on him. When he is nearly dry, you can take him out of the crate and brush him while the dryer is blowing the hair.

Hot Spots: If your dog has a thick coat or if the air is humid, blow-dryers are definitely preferred to air-drying. If your Berner isn't completely dried, he can develop *hot spots* overnight. Hot spots are places that dogs continually lick and scratch, and they can have many causes, including fleas, dry skin, infections, and allergies. The licking and scratching abrade the skin and can create an open wound that is hard to correct and heal. So make sure your dog is completely dry after his bath.

Ear Care

A clean, dry ear is more likely to stay healthy, so check and clean your Berner's ears regularly. Cleaning ears after a bath helps remove any water that collected there during bathing. If you see your dog scratching or flapping his ears, check and clean his ears. If the scratching persists, have your veterinarian check them.

- Clean his ear with a cotton ball dampened with ear cleaner, witch hazel, alcohol, or hydrogen peroxide. If there is any break in the skin, alcohol can sting, so select another alternative.
- Swab the inside of the earflap.
- Clean the dirt and wax from as much of the exposed ear as you can reach. You may have to squeeze the cotton ball to get into the crevasses.

• Ear care can include the trimming of the long stringy hairs, as described previously. You can also thin the hair on the inside of the earflap. On the other hand, you can leave the hair natural—your preference.

Dental Care

Keeping your Berner's teeth clean not only keeps him attractive, but can avoid bad breath and disease caused by poorly maintained teeth. Include weekly dental care in your grooming schedule. You can use a small soft toothbrush and special doggy toothpaste. In a pinch, a soft washcloth wrapped around your finger can substitute for a toothbrush and baking powder for toothpaste. The goal is to reduce tartar buildup that accumulates more quickly on his large molars that are near the salivary gland.

Chewing: Chewing may also help keep your Berner's teeth clean. Dry food's crunchiness helps and leaves less residue. Some large-dog-sized bones and chew toys can also contribute to keeping teeth clean and gums healthy. Make sure that he doesn't chew off a piece small enough to swallow.

Your veterinarian should examine your dog's teeth as part of his exam. He might recommend a deeper cleaning if there is significant tarter buildup. If you've noticed any loose, damaged, or different-colored teeth, point them out to your veterinarian. If puppy teeth have not fallen out when the adult teeth come in, your veterinarian can pull the puppy teeth.

Nail Trimming

Nail care is probably the grooming chore most disliked by both Berners and their owners, but it is very important and should be done every two weeks.

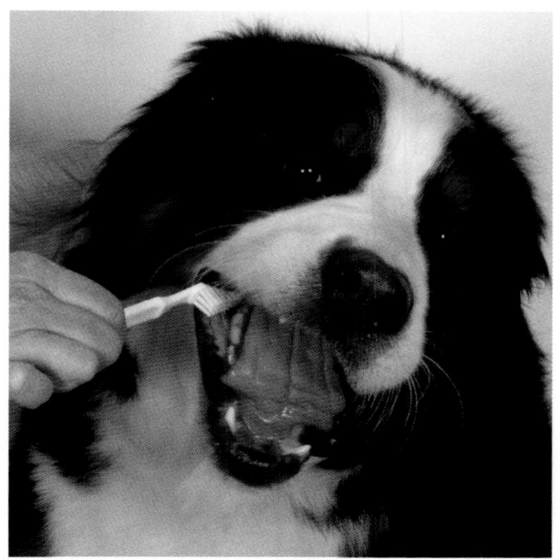

Regular dental care should be started when the Berner is a puppy so that he will accept such attention throughout his life.

It is easier to ignore long nails on a coated dog, but they harm him nonetheless. Long nails cause the dog to rock back on his feet. Rocking back causes the toes to spread and splay and become flat. Your Berner's feet are his support and his toes the shock absorbers. Your 100-pound (45-kg) dog needs good feet to carry him well and comfortably. Long nails can destroy the feet's ability to provide this function. If you can hear his nails on the floor, you have waited much too long.

The quick: Inside each nail is the quick, which contains blood vessels. If you allow the nail to grow long, the quick grows further out into the nail. This makes it harder to shorten the nails, for you may cut into the quick, which will bleed. This is an extra incentive to trim the nails regularly—to keep the quick from growing further into the nails.

TIP

Cut to the Quick

If you cut into the quick, you need to stop the bleeding. Styptic powder is available for this purpose. Put a small amount into a small bottle cap, then stick the bleeding nail into the small mound of powder to coat it to stop the bleeding. In a pinch, unflavored gelatin can substitute for styptic.

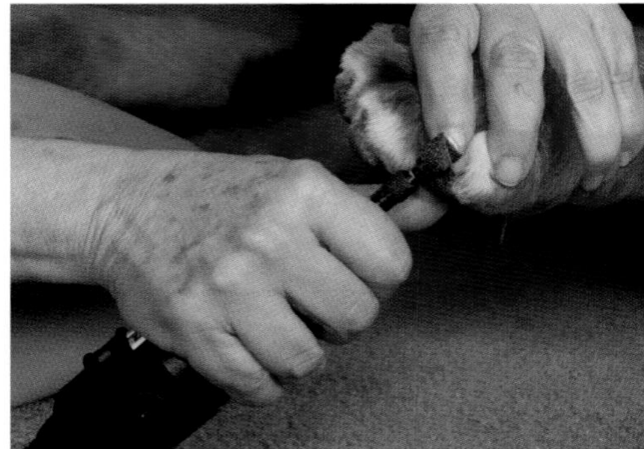

You are less likely to "quick" the dog's nails using a grinder. When you get close, the nail looks slightly pink.

Clippers and grinders: You can use a large nail clipper or a grinder to cut your Berner's nails. If you use a clipper, get one that is sized for large dogs. The grinders are electric tools with a small spinning paper sanding drum that files the dog's nails when touched against them. Grinders are more expensive, but dogs seem to mind them less, probably because the grinder doesn't pinch the nail. Make sure to use those made for grooming dogs.

✔ Trim excess hair on the feet first before using the grinder to get it out of the way. Work on the back feet first.
✔ Use the grinder on low speed.
✔ Touch the spinning grinder to the top end of the nail briefly multiple times in slightly different places to file off some with each touch.
✔ Don't leave the grinder on the nail too long, for it will get hot.

If your Berner has white nails, and many do, you can see to what point the quick extends and avoid trimming into it. If there are some dark nails, look underneath to see how far the "meat" extends. If you can trim the nails back to the quick each time, the quick will recede further back into the nail.

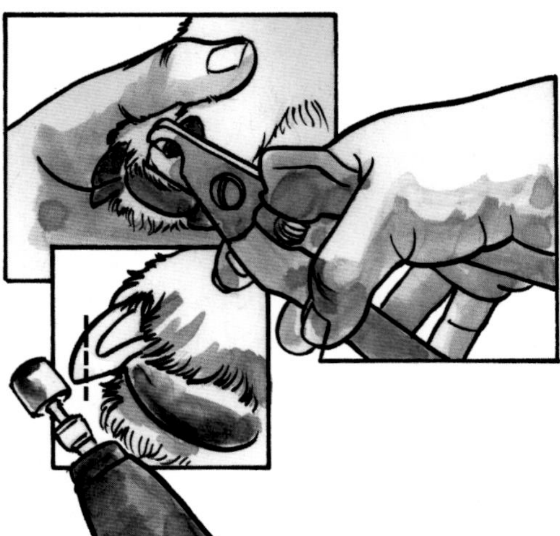

Whether using a clipper or grinder, you should trim your Berner's nails regularly to keep them short. Keep in mind that you should never hear the dog's nails click on the floor.

Your senior Berner still has plenty of coat to brush and should be groomed as regularly as one would a younger dog. But let him sit or lie down during grooming and keep the sessions short.

Dewclaws: Some breeders remove the dewclaws, vestigial toes on the inside of each leg above the paw. However, if they haven't, remember to trim those nails too.

If you don't want to trim your Berner's nails yourself, you can have your veterinarian or a groomer do it. Just make sure to have it done twice a month. Many veterinarians and groomers just take off the nail tip. Instruct them to trim the nail as short as possible without cutting into the quick. A groomer who works on show dogs and uses a grinder might take the best care of your dog's nails.

Many owners are overwhelmed at the thought of trimming their dog's nails, but it isn't difficult at all with a little practice. Start when your Berner is a puppy—smaller and easier to control. Puppies will protest the most, although some can be trained to cooperate with treats if you are patient and persistent. As dogs mature, they will accept the process more.

Senior Grooming

Consider the comfort of your older Berner during grooming. He won't be able to stand as long; the more that you can do with him sitting or lying down, the better. His coat may be drier and can benefit from a conditioner or creme rinse. Being less active, he won't help wear his nails down, so they may need trimming more often. You can break grooming activities into

Make walking your Berner a family affair. The exercise and fresh air is good for all of you.

shorter periods, allowing him time to rest or to go outside to relieve himself.

Exercise

The Bernese Mountain Dog is a working dog, used for centuries to help the Swiss farmer with his chores, including pulling carts. While some older dogs are more willing to be couch potatoes, younger Berners definitely need some vigorous activities to expend their energies. Some exercise tailored to the age of the dog is good for your Berner—and for you too.

Fences: A fenced yard with a sturdy fence is required for your dog. Berners aren't big climbers, so a 4- or 5-foot (1.2–1.5-m) fence will do. The yard needs to be big enough for him to run around in, especially when he is a youngster.

Walks: Neighborhood walks are great exercise for both of you. The distance should never be too long for the dog's strength, endurance, and age. Puppies need to be able to stop when they are tired, so keep the walks short unless you want to carry them home. Overexertion can stress young and rapidly growing bones and joints.

Adolescents and young adults can walk further and you will have a happier, more tired dog around your home. Seniors enjoy walks, too, but tailored to their capabilities. Some older Berners are in great athletic shape; others are feeling their age and can manage only shorter walks. Berners are people magnets. You won't be anonymous walking your handsome tricolored dog. People will want to visit and talk about your dog. On some walks, you may get more socializing done than exercise.

Heat

The heavy-coated Bernese Mountain Dog is most comfortable in cooler climates and revels in the cold and snow. During warmer times of year, and if you live in a warmer climate, schedule exercise only for the cooler times of the day—early morning or late at night. During the warmer parts of the day, he needs to be inside in the air conditioning.

From the many styles available, select dog beds that are soft, cushy, and easy to clean or launder.

Bedding

Your big dog deserves a comfortable soft bed. Beds come in many shapes and sizes. Get one that is large enough for the big dog your Berner puppy will become. It should be soft, too, to cushion young, and eventually, old bones and joints.

Get one that is easy to clean, perhaps with a removable cover that you can launder. If you sew, you can take a sheet, fold it in half top to bottom, and stitch the long edge and one short side, making a pillowcase-style cover. This can be used to cover a baby mattress or 4-inch-thick (10-cm) piece of foam to make a Berner bed.

Get a thick and comfortable pad for his crate, sized to fit the bottom. Fleece pads can be laundered and are a good choice if thick enough.

TIP

Don't Chew!

Teething puppies may chew their crate pads and bedding. While there are products available to keep puppies from chewing, spraying the edges and corners with an antiperspirant containing alum keeps the puppy from chewing them. Reapply after laundering.

A toy and a soft bed—life is good! Toys should be provided to accommodate the puppy's desire to chew during the teething stage. Food, dishes, toys, a collar and leash, and a bed should be purchased before the arrival of a new puppy.

YOUR INTELLIGENT BERNER

You found a beautiful Bernese Mountain Dog. You are caring for all her physical needs; now you need to tend to her inner dog, too—her intelligence, emotions, and character. The process will contribute to your relationship as best friends.

The Berner Character

Most Berners have a strong desire to please, but they like to do it in their own way. This makes them almost clownlike at times. They have a sensitive nature, though; strong-arm techniques and jerk-and-yank corrections won't work with them. They can seem stubborn about what things to do and how to do them. Remember, the many jobs they had on Swiss farms depended on their intelligence, responsibility, and independent action. They feel it is only reasonable to exercise those traits today, too.

Start training your puppy early. Dogs are learning all the time, beginning from the time their eyes and ears open. You can let them learn on their own, or you can guide them. The latter has huge benefits in your relationship and in having a dog that is better behaved and more civilized to live with. Even if you don't start with a puppy, "old" Berners can learn new tricks and more.

Just as her markings are both typical and unique, so is your Berner's personality. Treasure and enjoy her uniqueness, as you would want others to respect yours.

When training, consider the Bernese Mountain Dog character, developed as an all-purpose farm dog. As watchdogs on distant farms, they needed to be suspicious of strangers, and that nature can cause them to be wary of strangers today. They especially benefit from socialization as young puppies to learn to be comfortable around different people. A Berner that does not meet a great variety of people in many different settings as a youngster is likely to become a shy and distrustful adult.

They are not natural trackers or retrievers—those were not their jobs—but they can be trained to do both. They are very much into

Allowing your cute puppy on the furniture will eventually give permission to the large adult she will become to take her place on the couch.

people, and when petted may try to burrow into their laps. They can also keep their people company without being a pest. Left alone for extended periods, some may get into trouble. From their perspective, they are just looking for a job to do. Most of all, they want to be with their family.

TIP

Stages of Canine Development

0–13 days	Neonatal
13–21 days	Transition—ears and eyes open
21–23 days	Awareness—rapid sensory development
21–49 days	Socialization—puppy learns to be a dog
7–12 weeks	Socialization to people
8–10 weeks	Fear impact—trauma will have a lasting effect
4–8 months	Fear period—may become less confident with negative events
6–14 months	Second fear period—adolescence
18–24 months	Young adulthood

House Rules and House Manners

It's up to you to decide what you teach or fail to teach your Berner. The more you teach, the more she will be able to learn, the richer the relationship you two will have. You determine the house rules.

✔ Decide on your rules ahead of time so you can be consistent with your puppy.

✔ Don't let the puppy do anything you don't want the adult to do. If you don't want her on the furniture later, don't let the cute bundle of baby Berner on the furniture. It is entirely up to you whether your dog is allowed on the sofa or the bed or is permitted to get tidbits at the table. But don't allow it sometimes and then correct the same behavior later.

✔ Do not roughhouse with the puppy. When she grows into a strong adult, she will still want to play rough, and someone will get hurt. The Berner is a large, powerful working dog, and although she thinks she is playing, a person could get bruised or more.

Avoiding Problems

During house-training, limit the access your Berner puppy has to parts of your house. You wouldn't give a two-year-old toddler free, unsupervised access to your home. A puppy cannot handle that degree of freedom, either. Puppies get additional freedom as they earn it and can handle it. While she needs to be where the family is, she doesn't need to roam the entire house before she is reliable.

A crate is invaluable in training. With a soft mat, toys to play with, and something to chew, a puppy can be quite comfortable in a crate when a member of the family cannot watch her. You can also use an exercise pen (X-pen) to give her a larger area. An X-pen is a portable fence made of hinged panels that can corral her into or away from an area. If you have carpet, you can put a remnant of vinyl tile or a plastic tarp over the floor enclosed by the X-pen. Or you can use baby gates to keep your puppy in or out of a room.

A crate, X-pen, and baby gates allow you to avoid problems by controlling what your Berner has access to when you aren't watching. If she eats the plant, chews the sofa, or knocks over the lamp, you effectively allowed it. It is easier

Baby gates can help keep your Berner in or out of a room.

to plan ahead and avoid potential problems in the first place.

Digging

Berners like to dig. Maybe it is to find a cool place to lie down; maybe it is just the pleasure in the digging. You can consider a few options to control digging. You can accompany her each time she is outside and keep her busy with other activities so that she doesn't dig. If you are out with her, you can correct her when she starts digging.

An alternative is to give her a designated place in your yard to dig in, maybe even a sandbox for that purpose. You might bury a few bones or toys in that place so that she develops the habit of digging there, taking advantage of a dog's propensity to form and follow habits.

Take walks with your Berner and introduce her to friendly people, including different children, men, and women, providing positive learning experiences for all.

If she digs a hole that you don't want, you can put some of her fresh stool in the hole and cover it lightly with dirt. She won't dig in feces. Of course, she'll find another place to dig a hole.

No!

"*No*" is a word your dog needs to learn. It means, "Stop doing what you are doing now!" It should be said in a loud, stern, bossy voice. Your Berner understands tone of voice much better than the actual word. Don't overuse the word, however, or you will use up its value. If you say "*No*," "*No*," "*No*," "*No*" continuously, your dog will consider it nagging and will eventually ignore you. After you tell her "*No*!" give her an alternative that you find acceptable, such as a toy to play with or a bone to chew.

Socialization

Socialization is important for all dogs. Its goal is to create a dog that is happy and confidant and that expects the world to be a friendly place. It is especially important for the Bernese Mountain Dog that can become shy if kept isolated and not provided with the opportunity to meet new people, places, and dogs and to have new experiences.

While socialization continues throughout the life of the dog, you can make the most impact with your Berner by doing a great deal of social-

Places to Go, Things to Do

- Neighborhood walks
- Pet superstore
- Puppy kindergarten classes
- Dog obedience classes—sit out of the way and watch
- Car trips
- Parks
- Kennel
- Groomer
- Your or other places of business (if allowed)
- Veterinarian
- Vacation
- Playgrounds (if allowed)
- Dog shows
- Dog beaches
- Little League and other sporting games
- Agility classes—sit and watch
- Assisted living and nursing homes
- Picnics
- Neighbors' homes and yards (if allowed)
- Other family members' homes and yards (if allowed)
- On sidewalks of strip malls
- Parades

ization from age seven weeks to four months. At this time, she is a sponge, and experiences will have the most impact. Something new daily is ideal or at least several new experiences each week. Take her with you whenever possible.

The socialization mustn't be indiscriminate, however. Make sure that every new experience is a positive one. Negative experiences may affect lifelong attitudes just as positive ones can. Make sure that all the people she meets are friendly and treat her gently and kindly. Include senior citizens, children, teenagers, men, women, and people of different races, sizes, and postures among her new acquaintances. Prescreen all dogs you want her to meet for friendliness. Don't let any big dogs jump on or frighten her, even in play, or you may find later that she is aggressive to that kind of dog.

If she isn't always confident in a new situation, don't calm her in a soothing voice. Doing so reinforces the fearful response. Ignore her fear, but don't push her. Just be brave and confident and friendly yourself. She will look to you, her leader. If you act like there is nothing wrong, she will come to that conclusion, too, and become more comfortable in the situation.

Never leave your Berner in an enclosed, unventilated car. Dogs don't have an efficient system to cool themselves, can easily become overheated, and may even get sick or die.

How Dogs Learn

To train your Berner, you need to understand how she learns. Dogs, like us, do what feels good and is rewarding and avoid what doesn't feel good. Your challenge is to make what you want her to do seem rewarding to her.

Some people feel that petting and praise are sufficient to reward a dog's performance. Would you work for a boss who only paid you with a "Thank you"? No, you want a paycheck. Your dog's paycheck is treats, extra tasty treats such as meat and cheese. The main criterion is that your dog loves the treat and will do whatever you want her to do to get it.

Use the treat to get your Berner to do the behavior you want, such as *sit*, *down*, or *come*, without touching her, if possible. Urge her to do it without using a command—she doesn't know the word. You can hold the treat above her nose to get her to sit. When she starts to or does sit, give her a treat and tell her what a good girl she is. Repeat until she sees that the behavior gets her the treat. After she is reliably doing the behavior (sitting), then you can say the word "*Sit*" each time you have her perform, still using the treat, and attach the command to the action.

Train Positively

✔ Keep training sessions frequent and fun, but short. A few minutes are sufficient to get your puppy to perform a behavior a time or two and treat and praise her. Ten five-minute sessions each day is better than one hour-long session.

✔ Have her do a behavior that you are practicing before she gets each meal. This brings to life the motto "Will work for food."

✔ When dogs learn a behavior, they learn it in the context it was taught. So, if you taught *sit* in the living room, the behavior is connected with the living room. Include different locations in your training, so your Berner knows *sit-in-the-bedroom*, *sit-in-the-kitchen*, and *sit-in-the-front-yard* as well as *sit-in-the-living-room*.

✔ Be consistent with your commands. Decide on one word for each command, and use only that word. When you want your dog to come, don't say "*Come*" sometimes, "*Here*" other times, and "*Come here*" on occasion, too.

✔ Train positively, making it fun for your puppy. If you are harsh with her, your Berner will shut down and won't learn. Your dog won't respond to jerk-and-yank handling or prong collars. Your training time should be fun for both of you, a time to enhance your relationship and bond.

TIP

Five Seconds

Five seconds—that is the time limit you have to offer a treat to reinforce a behavior or give a correction to discourage a behavior. Ideally, treat and praise or correct while the behavior is happening. After five seconds, your dog won't know what she is being praised or punished for.

Basic Obedience

In order to train your puppy, first you must have her attention. Your Berner is paying attention to you when she is looking at you. The following fun exercise can teach attention.

Attention

Get some very tasty treats and have some in each of your closed hands so the puppy cannot get it. Sit or kneel in front of your puppy so she can easily look at you. If working with an adult dog, you can stand. Let the puppy know you have treats in your hands. Hold your hands about 2 feet (61 cm) apart a bit higher than your puppy's head. She will try to get the treats from your hands, but don't let her. Tease her by letting her sniff your treat-containing hands to keep her interested.

She will eventually make eye contact with you as she tries to figure how to get the goodies. The instant she looks in your eyes, even for a second, give her a treat, and tell her "*Good Girl*!" Each time she makes eye contact, give her a treat and praise again. Alternate hands giving the treat so that she doesn't know which one the treat comes from.

Pretty soon, she will figure it out and stare at you, since it is the eye contact that is making the treat appear. After she gets the concept, you can attach a command to the behavior, such as "*Watch Me*" or "*Ready*." Now she is ready for further instruction, for she is paying attention to you.

What you want to teach your Berner is up to you. *Attention* and *Sit* are very useful and described previously. Most want their dogs to *Come* when called. *Down* and *Stay* are also handy for companion dogs.

Recall

Having your dog come when called is convenient and can be critical. Crouch down, hold out your arms and the treat, and call your dog's name and say "*Come.*" Be enthusiastic and happy and encouraging. When she comes, praise and pet her and give her wonderful treats. Keep treats in your pockets; several times a day, call your Berner to you, offering love and petting and more treats.

Coming to you must always be a wonderful experience for your dog. Never, *ever* call her to you to do anything she doesn't like, such as getting a bath or having her nails trimmed. Don't ever, ever call her to you to correct her, no matter what she has done. If you do, you are teaching her *not* to come to you. If you need her for grooming or medicine, go get her.

Down

We discussed the *sit* command above. *Down* can be taught when your Berner is in the *sit* position. Put a treat in front of her nose and move it toward the floor at an angle. As she follows it down with her nose, when her elbows touch the ground, praise her and give her the treat. If her rump comes off the ground, don't give her the treat. Have her sit again, and try again to lure her into the *down* position.

Stay

Stay is a different command; you are asking your dog not to do something, to not move.

As the leader, it is your responsibility to ensure that training is both fun and rewarding for your dog.

The secret is to do it in tiny steps. Have your dog *sit*. Then ask her to *stay*, and count to five. When done, release her with the word "*Okay,*" give her a treat, and tell her how good she is. When she will *stay* for a count of five, count to ten. If she gets up, have her *sit* again, and start over. When she will stay sitting next to you for

To train your dog, you must first have her attention. You know you have her attention when she is looking at you and waiting for your communication.

a count of 30, have her sit, tell her "*Stay*," and pivot so that you are standing in front of her. Since you've changed your location, start with the low count of five again. Proceed until she can do it longer with you in front.

When she has the concept of *stay*, tell her "*Stay*" and take a step away. Again, you have changed the context, in this case the distance, so go back to the shorter time you are asking her to *stay*. You can increase time or distance, but not both at the same time. Make sure you say your release word "*Okay*" so she knows when she can move. And remember to reward her each time with a treat.

Distractions

It is wonderful for your dog to behave in your home, to *come*, *sit*, *down*, and *stay* on command. But you cannot consider a behavior reliable until your Berner can do it with distractions.

When you are confident she knows the commands, practice them outside your home, on the sidewalk, in a park, during a walk. Keep the lead on to make sure you have control. Practice the commands when there are other people, including children and animals, around.

You can add distractions in your home, too. Have her *down* and *stay*, and rap on some surface. Toss a ball or bone or toy in the air or drop one on the floor. For the ultimate test, ring the doorbell. Practice with distractions until you can count on her behaving.

Training and learning are lifelong processes. At this point, you have made a good start. The more your Berner learns, the more she can learn.

Classes and Trainers

Training classes are among the many places you can take your Berner. Many area obedience clubs offer a variety of classes taught by their members who have trained and earned titles with their dogs. Large dogs need training, for they will be harder to control if untrained when

Berners are working dogs who need something interesting to do. Pulling carts and sleds is a wonderful form of exercise.

grown than a smaller dog. Newer owners can greatly benefit from the expertise of experienced trainers. Classes have the benefit of training the dog to do his exercises away from home and among other people and dogs as well as at home with the family.

One of the first to pursue is Puppy Kindergarten. This is a class for young puppies to learn through games and to meet other people and other dogs. It is gentle training geared to a puppy's energy level and attention span. It is a great opportunity for your puppy to continue to learn how to learn.

Many clubs also offer multiple levels of obedience classes, such as basic, intermediate, and advanced. Training is available for those who want a well-behaved companion as well as for people who want to compete with their dogs in performance events.

You may visit the clubs or schools that offer training classes to watch before signing up. You want trainers who train with positive methods and encourage using toys or treats as well as verbal praise. Consider training methods, class size, and what is taught in the class. Select the classes that best suit you and your dog.

TO HIS HEALTH

We each want a long, happy, and healthy life for our Bernese. His chances are greatly improved with an observant and knowledgeable owner and a competent veterinarian. An old Swiss saying claims, "Three years a young dog, three years a good dog, three years an old dog. All else is a gift from God." With good care, your Berner can be healthy and comfortable for those years, and with some luck, for more years after that.

Choosing a Veterinarian

Find your veterinarian before you need her, ideally before you get your dog.

Veterinarians vary in their levels of expertise and experience. You want one who is very knowledgeable about large dogs, especially about those medical conditions that may affect Bernese Mountain Dogs. The more she knows, the more accurate her diagnoses will be, and therefore the more effective your dog's treatment. So, how do you find this medical paragon?

If you are fortunate enough to live near your Bernese Mountain Dog's breeder, consider using the veterinarian he uses. The veterinarian knows your breeder's dogs and perhaps other Berners in her practice. If your breeder recommends his veterinarian, you would do well to go to her if she is within a reasonable distance.

Your Berner can credit his good health to good genes from his parents and good care from a responsible and vigilant owner (you) and a knowledgeable and expert veterinarian.

If your breeder and his veterinarian aren't nearby, identify veterinarians that show-dog breeders and owners use, especially breeders and owners with Berners or other large dogs. People with show dogs usually have more dogs and therefore use their veterinarians' services more often. They also talk to each other and share their experiences about different veterinarians.

✔ Several resources can help you find the show dog and Berner people near you. Your breeder may know other Berner owners in your area. The BMDCA has members throughout the country; some may live near you or know

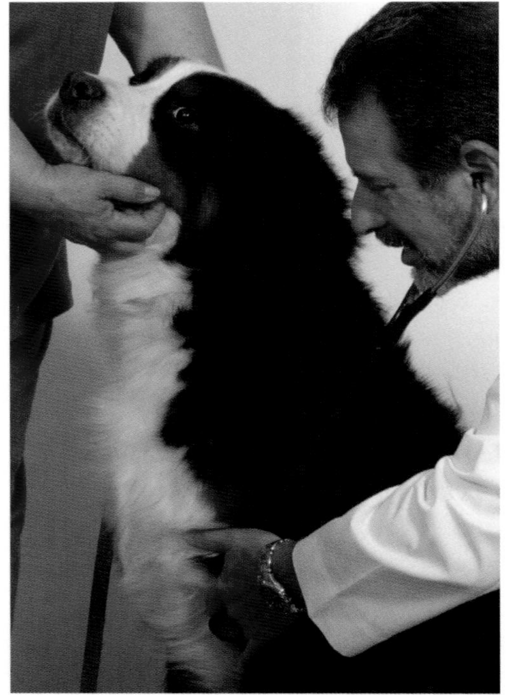

Schedule an annual appointment for your Berner with your veterinarian for a thorough check-up.

others who do. Your local kennel club, which you can find on AKC's Web site, has members who may help you. See the chapter *Finding a Bernese Mountain Dog* for information about and accessing the BMDCA and AKC Web sites.

✔ Go to shows in your area. You can find shows, dates, and locations on AKC's Web site, also.

✔ Ask the local people you meet who have Bernese and other large dogs which veterinarians they go to.

Note the veterinarians who are recommended by multiple people; make appointments and visit them. Tell them that you will be getting a Bernese Mountain Dog. Ask what advice they have to keep your dog in good health. Ask what health issues affect Berners and what the recommended treatments are. Also inquire about how they handle emergencies, since most dogs don't conveniently get sick during office hours. Most veterinarians today do not handle their own emergencies if there is an emergency clinic available.

Select a veterinarian who has the competence you want and with whom you have the best rapport, one who will explain things to you and who listens to what you say. Remember that the best veterinarian may not be the one closest to your home. It is worth the extra trouble to find the best veterinarian that you can. The payoff is a healthier Bernese.

The Observant Owner

You are your Berner's first line of defense. Your job is to notice any changes in him that might indicate a problem. Dogs are creatures of habit. It is up to you to see anything he does differently that might be a sign of illness. See the end of the chapter for details on monitoring your dog's health.

Breed-Specific Health Issues

Some breeds have a higher incidence of specific health problems. A knowledgeable owner must be familiar with these problems, their symptoms, and their treatment. Early detection may offer the most treatment options.

Discuss Bernese health issues with your breeder. He can share his experiences and knowledge with you on what to look for and the health care he has found successful. Your carefully selected veterinarian is another primary resource in identifying problems and in explaining the treatment choices best suited for you and your dog.

Cancer

All dogs can get cancer, including the Bernese Mountain Dog. Among the cancers more common in Berners are histiocytosis and mast cell tumors. According to the 2005 BMDCA health survey, 15 percent of Berners get some kind of tumor and almost one quarter of those have histiocytosis. This is a relatively rare disease that occurs more frequently among Bernese Mountain Dogs.

Histiocytosis

There are several versions of histiocytosis. The malignant forms are often fatal. Histiocytes are a type of white blood cells that migrate into body tissue and have a normal function in the canine immune system. Histiocytosis occurs when the cells reproduce abnormally. There are different opinions on how separate and distinct the types of histiocytosis are; your veterinarian can tell you his current understanding of the disease and the treatment options available.

Systemic histiocytosis involves multiple masses that may occur anyplace, but are usually found on the skin of the head and extremities. It may go into remission, but later recur. It may spread to other organs, such as the spleen, liver, bone marrow, or lungs. There has been some success treating this condition with immunosuppressive drugs.

TIP

Common Signs of Canine Cancer

- ✔ Disinterest in exercise; lack of energy.
- ✔ Abnormal swellings that last or continue to grow.
- ✔ Bad odor.
- ✔ Poor appetite.
- ✔ Sores that don't heal.
- ✔ Unexplained weight loss.
- ✔ Continuing lameness or stiffness.
- ✔ Bleeding or discharge from any orifice.
- ✔ Problems breathing, urinating, or defecating.
- ✔ Difficulty eating or swallowing.

Malignant histiocytic sarcoma is an aggressive cancer. It may be widespread in the body before any symptoms are noticed. This cancer affects many organs simultaneously. When many organs are involved, surgery isn't a viable

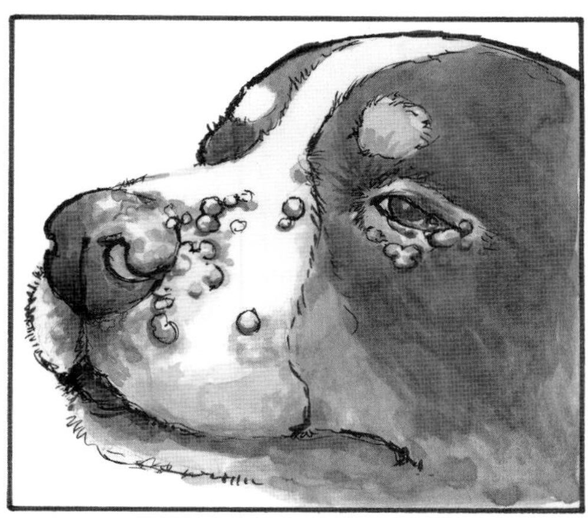

An example of a dog with malignant histiocytic sarcoma.

A happy expression may reflect a healthy dog, but to be sure, feel all over your dog's body weekly, checking for anything that might be a problem.

option. There is no current treatment for the malignant version, other than homeopathic remedies. Survival after diagnosis seldom extends beyond a few weeks.

Malignant histiocytosis should not be confused with a benign form of histiocytic disease. Histiocytoma is a small growth found on or under the skin. The lump will be about the size of your fingertip. It may go away by itself in a few weeks, or it may remain. Either way, it is harmless.

Mast Cell Tumor

Mast cells are a type of cell in the dermis, the thicker portion of the skin. When these cells

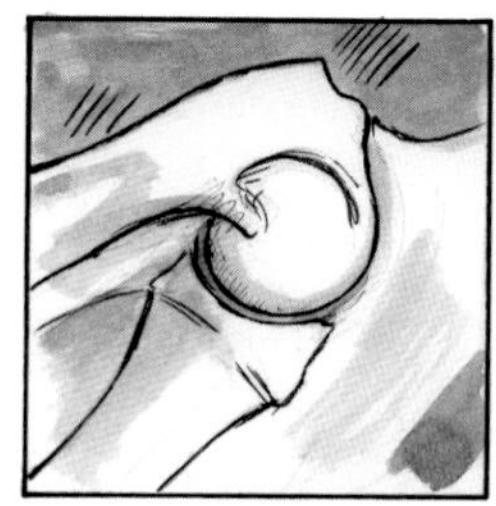

The left elbow joint is normal; the elbow joint on the right is dysplastic.

grow out of control, they produce a mast cell tumor. A quarter of all canine skin tumors are mast cell tumors; half of these are malignant. About half of the mast cell tumors are located on the body, many on the legs, and a few on the head or neck. Most are found on the skin, although they can be anywhere. They can occur at any age, but most develop in older dogs.

Check your dog regularly for lumps. If you find one, have it checked by your veterinarian. She can determine if it is cancerous and what the treatment options are. Surgery, chemotherapy, and or radiation may be considered. The choices may depend on how localized or widespread the tumor or cancer is and how aggressive or fast growing it is estimated to be. The location of the tumor can also affect the options.

Skeletal System Issues

Many large breeds, including Bernese, are susceptible to bone problems. There are both hereditary and environmental components. Discuss with your breeder the health problems she has experienced with her dogs, the remedies she has found effective, and the health tests she has done on them. Ideally, both parents have been evaluated clear of both elbow and hip dysplasia by OFA (Orthopedic Foundation for Animals). PennHip is another method of evaluating hips, and measures joint laxity; it is a rigorous procedure that can only be done by certified PennHip veterinarians. You can help avoid problems by feeding your dog appropriately, providing proper bedding, and monitoring his exercise to avoid trauma and injury, especially when he is growing and his skeletal system is developing (see chapter *Caring for Your Berner*).

Elbow Dysplasia

Elbow dysplasia (ED) is a term for several developmental degenerative diseases of the elbow. Based on Berners evaluated from 1974 through 2005, OFA elbow evaluation statistics report nearly 30 percent of Bernese Mountain Dogs affected.

The elbow joint is formed at the juncture of three bones: the humerus of the upper arm and the radius and ulna of the forearm. Current thought is that problems are caused by improper growth or shape of the bones, the bones growing at different rates, or by injury that affects the bone growth. There are different types of elbow dysplasia depending on where the fault lies.

Joint incongruity is the term used when the radius and ulna don't grow at the same rate. The bone that grows more slowly can cause the other bone to curve, which causes the end of the curved bone to not fit into the elbow properly.

Ununited anconeal process is a condition where a portion of the end of the ulna doesn't properly fit into the matching end of the humerus. A piece of bone may detach and float in the joint, causing pain.

While Berner owners should be aware of health issues found in the breed, the vast majority of Bernese Mountain Dogs will encounter none of these conditions and will enjoy good health.

Fragmented coronoid process is a condition caused by the improper development of the groove (trochlear notch) in the head of the ulna where the humerus fits. This causes too much weight to be put on the edge of the notch, causing it to fracture.

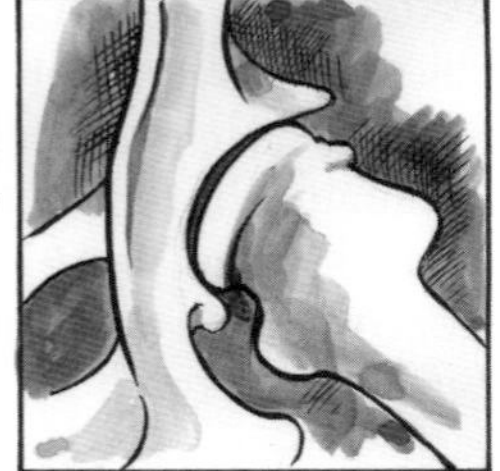

Most elbow joint problems occur as the puppy grows. They can be mild to severe, depending on how much change there is in the bones. Discuss treatment options with your veterinarian, which may include surgery for some serious cases or medications to reduce inflammation and pain and to lubricate the joint. Veterinary understanding of elbow dysplasia is continually changing, so the treatment choices and benefits are changing, too.

Hip Dysplasia

The hip joint is a ball-and-socket joint. The head of the femur or thighbone is the ball that fits into the socket or acetabulum of the pelvis. When the formation of the head of the femur or the socket is misshapen or if they fit poorly, the dog has hip dysplasia (HD). OFA current statistics report almost 17 percent of the Berners tested having HD. HD is diagnosed with an X-ray. The dog must be positioned properly to get an accurate picture of the hip joint. If the dog is not in the correct position, hip dysplasia may be diagnosed when the dog does not have it.

A dog may have hip dysplasia and have no symptoms at all, while other dogs are more seriously affected. The condition gets progressively worse as the dog ages, with arthritic changes in the imperfectly formed and fitting joint. The dog may eventually limp, avoid exercise, or have trouble getting up.

The cause of hip dysplasia is unknown, but there is definitely a hereditary component. Bernese breeders should have their dogs' hips

The hip joint on the left is formed more normally than the dysplastic hip joint on the right.

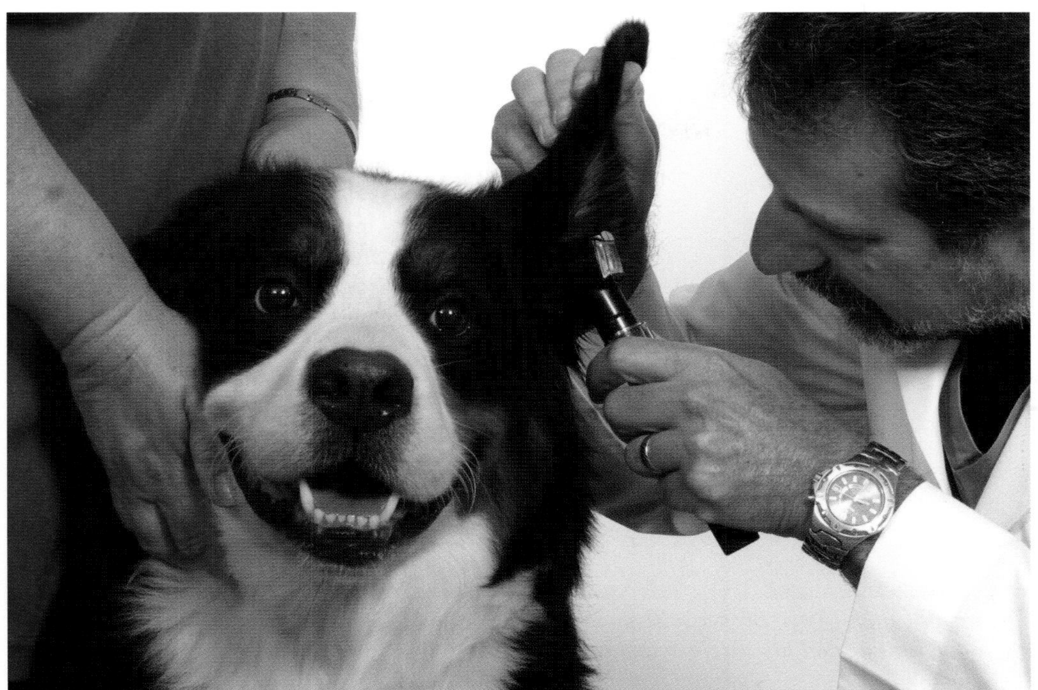

Your veterinarian will examine your dog's ears as part of the annual check-up. Tell your veterinarian if your dog has been rubbing or scratching his ears.

evaluated by OFA or PennHip. But even parents that test clear can produce an offspring with hip problems.

Care: Your care of your puppy can also reduce the chance of his developing HD, and other bone problems as well. Keep your puppy slender as his bones are developing—overweight puppies and adolescents are twice as likely to have bad hips. High-calorie diets, excessive calcium, and an unbalanced calcium-phosphorus ratio increase the risk of HD. While youngsters need free exercise, avoid prolonged excessive exercise, especially the type that can produce trauma or injury, which can put too much stress on developing bones and joints. Wait until he is at least a year and a half old before trying obedience jumps or heavy drafting work.

Treatment: Many dogs can function and enjoy life with HD and elbow dysplasia, as people do with arthritis. If your Berner has significant symptoms, discuss treatment options with a qualified orthopedic veterinarian. While surgical treatment is hard on a large dog and should be considered only in more severe cases, it may make the difference between moderate and severe symptoms. You can consider medications to reduce inflammation and pain and to lubricate the joint.

The good health of your Berner will show in his eyes and expression, his lustrous coat and muscular fitness, and his carriage and attitude.

Osteoarthritis

Osteoarthritis is a general term for degenerative joint problems. The cause may be trauma or genetic. Many dogs are affected by osteoarthritis, especially as they age.

Normal joints have smooth cartilage that covers the ends of bones. Cartilage plus joint fluid provides for comfortable functioning of the joints. If a joint is damaged or incorrectly formed, the cartilage will become rough. Joint fluid may be lost. Your dog will experience pain when moving the joint. Osteoarthritis can result from the hip and elbow dysplasia described previously, but it is not limited to those joints.

The joints involved and the severity of the condition will determine the available treatments. Your veterinarian can list the options and can recommend those she thinks have the best prognosis. Sometimes, surgery is advised. Often, pain management, reduction of inflammation, and use of medications to increase joint fluids are the appropriate prescriptions. Allowing exercise that the dog is able and willing to do and keeping the dog slender will also help your Bernese.

Bone Problems of Large-Puppy Development

Berner puppies grow fast, reaching most of their adult height in the first year. As a result, they may encounter one of the bone diseases that are sometimes seen in large breeds. Excessive and unbalanced calcium and high-calorie foods can cause or contribute to bone problems. Keeping a puppy slim can reduce stress on his growing bones and limit the problems.

Panosteitis ("pano") or wandering lameness is a disease that affects large puppies between five and twelve months old. Males are affected more often than females. A characteristic of pano is the pain and lameness shifting from one leg to another over some weeks or months. Your veterinarian may recommend medication be given for pain. Exercise may be limited until the puppy grows through the disease, which is self-limiting. The cause of the condition isn't known.

Osteochondrosis (OCD) is a condition caused by a defect in normal cartilage formation during rapid skeletal growth. Pieces of cartilage may break off and cause joint pain and swelling. It often occurs in the joint between the shoulder and upper arm and may also occur in the elbow and other joints. It tends to happen between four and eight months of age. The puppy is lame and gets worse with exercise. An irregular or loose piece of cartilage may show up on an X-ray. Restricting activity and medication for pain can help your Berner. Drugs, including Adequan, are now being used to resolve the problem without surgery. In some cases, surgery may be necessary to remove the piece of cartilage. Your veterinarian can recommend the appropriate choices if your Berner gets this condition.

Hypertrophic Osteodystrophy (HOD) is characterized by inflammation of the growth plates at the ends of the bones, usually the lower leg. It affects large breed puppies between two and eight months. A fever, depression, and weight loss may accompany it. X-rays can confirm the diagnosis, and your veterinarian will discuss the treatment options available. Cases that seem to be impacted by excess diet calcium or calories should be helped by change in diet. Treatment can include medications to relieve pain. Antibiotics may be given if there is an infection. While HOD is very painful, the dog can recover with treatment.

An eye with cataracts may have a cloudy appearance on the lens.

Eye Problems

There are several eye problems that may occur in Bernese. Yearly eye exams can check for the various types that may affect Bernese Mountain Dogs.

Cataracts may appear in puppies or young dogs as well as in aging dogs. Cataracts are a breakdown of the lens of the eye that becomes less transparent and therefore impairs vision. Depending on the severity, your veterinarian may recommend surgery, which is normally very successful.

Progressive retinal atrophy (PRA) is a general term for hereditary diseases of the eye, specifically of the retina that is at the back of

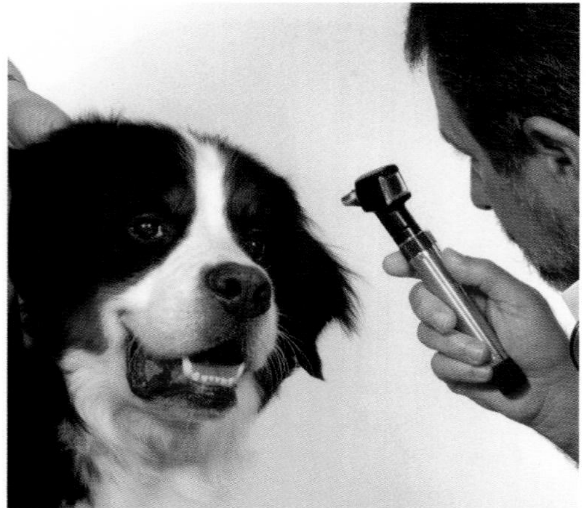

While your veterinarian will check your Berner's eyes during the annual check-up, it does not replace a more thorough exam by a veterinary ophthamologist.

the inside of the eye. A dog with PRA develops difficulty seeing and eventually goes blind. With a little training and management, most dogs can adjust to the lack of sight.

Although not a frequent problem, early-onset PRA has been found in some Bernese Mountain Dogs. It can be identified early after birth, with complete blindness usually occurring at from one to five years. It is hereditary and recessive, so both parents must carry it for their puppy to be affected. Late-onset PRA may also affect Berners, with blindness occurring some time after three years of age.

Entropion is the abnormal rolling in of the eyelid so that eyelashes irritate the surface of the eye. It causes excessive tearing and may at some point damage the eye. Your veterinarian may treat the condition by pulling the offending lashes if the problem is minor or may recommend surgery if the problem is more severe.

Ectropion is a condition where the lower eyelid turns outward. There may be no symptoms, or there may be tearing and infection.

If your dog's eyes seem to be irritated and red or if they tear more than normal, you should ask your veterinarian to check for entropion or ectropion.

All Bernese should get an annual eye exam by a veterinary ophthalmologist. Results should be forwarded to Canine Eye Registry Foundation (CERF). Many dog clubs offer eye clinics, often called CERF clinics, at dog shows and matches where the exam can be done relatively inexpensively.

Bloat and Torsion

Bloat occurs when gas builds up in a dog's stomach causing it to expand or bloat. The bloated stomach may twist or torsion. The torsion closes the stomach off from the esophagus and small intestine and cuts off the stomach's blood supply. The dog is in pain and will go into shock; the stomach tissue begins dying, and if untreated, the dog will die.

Be familiar with the symptoms so you will recognize bloat immediately. The dog will most likely retch and have dry heaves, but all that comes up is a yellow or pale frothy, viscous mucous. His back may be hunched; he may pant in distress. A bloating dog's stomach will feel taut, like a basketball. He may appear to be uncomfortable, so that he tries to lie down, only to get up, pace, and then try to lie down again.

If you suspect that your dog is bloating, you must get him to a veterinarian immediately. You cannot delay even an hour; if you delay, your dog may die. The veterinarian will treat your dog for shock and take steps to decom-

TIP

Signs of Bloat

The sooner you can identify bloat, the sooner you can seek help. Your dog may not have all these symptoms, but still be bloated.

- Unproductive and repeated vomiting, producing only mucous or froth.
- Timpanic-feeling stomach, like a drum.
- Distended stomach, enough to see the swelling.
- Salivating, panting, whining.
- Inability to get comfortable.
- Depressed.
- Standing with head hanging, back slightly arched.
- Pale gums (a later symptom indicating poor circulation).
- Lying down on elbows and rear feet to reduce pressure on belly.

press the stomach. If the dog has torsioned, surgery is necessary to untwist and empty the stomach. During surgery, the veterinarian should tack (suture) the dog's stomach to the side of his abdominal cavity to prevent it from twisting again.

Sometimes when the stomach twists, the spleen also torsions. The spleen can also torsion independently, without the stomach being involved. In either case, the spleen can be removed with no harm to the dog, as the liver can assume the functions of the spleen. Before removing the spleen, confirm that your veterinarian knows that it should be taken out *without* untwisting it. If the spleen is untwisted, the

The pattern formed by the white hair on the Berner's neck and chest is sometimes said to resemble an inverted cross.

toxic buildup will be released, and the dog will probably die.

Cause

The cause of bloat is unknown. It is recommended that a dog not exercise an hour before and after eating. Dogs fed smaller meals more frequently—at least twice a day—have a lower incidence of bloat. Some suspect that dogs gulp air as they eat. Putting the dog food on the floor, rather than elevated, may slow a fast eater and limit the gulping. Stress probably contributes to bloat. The calmer your dog is before, during, and after each meal, the more likely his digestive system will function properly. If you think your dog is gassy and may bloat, you can give him a liquid anti-gas product available from your drugstore that is primarily simethicone.

Discuss current vaccine protocols with your veterinarian. Required vaccines and how often they are given may vary according to where you live and the current science.

Hopefully your dog won't bloat. But observe your dog to recognize it if it does happen. You know more now and can provide help for your dog when he needs it.

von Willebrand's Disease (vWD)

Von Willebrand's Disease is a form of bleeder's disease. It impairs the ability of the blood to clot, and an affected dog can bleed to death from an incision that would normally cause no problem. It is at least partially hereditary. The condition can vary from mild to severe, depending on the degree to which the Berner is affected with the von Willebrand's factor, which is used by the blood in the clotting process. There is a simple test that can be done prior to surgery to determine if the dog has vWD. If he does, your veterinarian will need to have a clotting medicine available.

Vaccines and Prevention

Diseases that killed dogs a few decades ago now have vaccines available. Your Berner puppy will have gotten his initial vaccines while with his breeder. When you first visit your veterinarian with your new puppy, take with you a record of the inoculations he has had so far. Your veterinarian will recommend a series of vaccines and when they should be administered. Failure to vaccinate can risk disease, but overvaccination also has risks, including a negative reaction your pet may have to the injection. Opinions on the best protocols for providing immunity at lower risk are evolving; ask your veterinarian what the latest recommendations and options are.

Vaccines today are categorized as *core* and *noncore*. The core vaccines protect against diseases that are very serious and potentially fatal. They include canine parvovirus (CPV), canine distemper virus (CDV), canine adenovirus (CAV), and rabies. Noncore vaccines are for diseases that are less serious, easily treated, or self-limiting, or that your puppy has little risk of contracting. These vaccines include those for canine parainfluenza virus (CPiV), distemper-measles combination, bordatella, leptospirosis, and Lyme disease.

Heartworm

If there are mosquitoes in your area, your Bernese must be on heartworm preventative. When a mosquito carrying heartworm bites your dog, the heartworm larvae are transmitted to the dog. The larvae develop in the body for several months and end up as adult heartworms in the dog's heart and lungs. They can eventually kill a dog.

While heartworm can be treated, it is expensive and hard on the dog. It is far better to give your dog regular heartworm prevention medicine. There are a variety of options for heartworm prevention, including monthly tablets and chewables and monthly topicals. They are extremely effective, and when they are given on a timely schedule, heartworm infection is completely avoidable. Any dog that is not on heartworm preventative must be checked for heartworms before starting it.

Parasites—Internal and External

Fleas and ticks are the most bothersome external parasites. They not only annoy you and your Berner and cause skin problems, but they also carry disease. If you have them, you must simultaneously treat the dog, your home, and your yard.

Flea collars aren't very effective on Bernese Mountain Dogs because the dog is too large for the flea collar to completely protect him, and his thick coat prevents the collar from being in contact with the skin. Topical products available from your veterinarian are effective against fleas on your dog. When treating the house and yard, make sure the product kills both the adult fleas and ticks and also the eggs. If you do not, in two weeks, you will have a new infestation.

Finding fleas and ticks is a challenge on the thick black coat of your Berner. A flea comb helps locate the fleas. When looking for ticks, make sure you examine you dog's head, inside and behind his ears, where his legs join his body, and on his feet: between his toes and around the pads. You will need to look and feel through the coat in order to locate ticks.

Internal parasites are primarily intestinal worms: hookworms, tapeworms, roundworms, and whipworms. Often, but not always, when the dog has these worms, your veterinarian can detect them by examining a stool sample under a microscope. You may be able to see bits of white tapeworm (about a quarter to a half inch in length) in your dog's stool. If your Berner has diarrhea, have your dog checked for worms or infection. Intestinal worms are usually easily treatable. Depending on the product used, the heartworm prevention medication may take care of intestinal worms other than tapeworms.

TIP

Removing Fleas and Ticks

Rubbing alcohol is toxic to both fleas and ticks. If you find a flea on your dog, you can spray it with rubbing alcohol. If you find a tick attached to your dog, you can spray it with alcohol first to loosen its grip. Then grab it next to the dog's skin with tweezers, pull it off slowly, and drop it into a bit of alcohol. Remove it slowly so that the head of the tick doesn't detach and remain attached to the dog.

TIP

Fighting Fleas

Put a flea collar in your vacuum cleaner bag to help you combat this parasite. Remember to replace it with a new one periodically.

Pets should be spayed or neutered when they are about one year old. The hormones they have prior to being altered help them develop and mature properly.

Pick up and dispose of your dog's feces to help avoid spreading worms. Have your dog's stool examined as part of his yearly health checkup.

Spaying and Neutering

If you purchased your Berner as a pet, it is strongly recommended that the males are neutered and the females are spayed. Neutering the males avoids their getting testicular cancer and reduces the incidence of prostate cancer. Spaying the females protects them from uterine cancer and serious uterine infections such as pyometra or endometriosis and lowers the risk of breast cancer.

There are many opinions on when to get your Bernese spayed or neutered. Some veterinarians recommend it be done as puppies. Others believe that early spaying or neutering before sexual maturity may have negative effects on the dog's growth and may even contribute to future problems. Talk to both your dog's breeder and your veterinarian to make an informed decision.

When a dog is spayed or neutered, it no longer has the sex hormones that can affect behavior, but it does not change your dog's personality. Contrary to common opinion, spaying and neutering doesn't make your dog fat—too much food and too little exercise makes your dog fat.

Time to Say Good-bye

At some point, it will be time to say good-bye to your Bernese Mountain Dog. Some dogs pass on their own. Some are lost suddenly and unexpectedly. Others grow older and acquire symptoms of advanced age and sometimes a debilitating disease. While not pleasant, euthanasia may be the final gift you can give him in return for all the love he has given you.

It may be hard to decide when to have it done. It should be determined by the quality of life the dog has. He doesn't have to be as athletic as a youngster to have a quality life. If he enjoys the warmth of the sun, being near you, getting a cookie, and is not in much pain, he has a good life. But when pain from disease or age is substantial enough to prevent any pleasure, it is time. A small dog that cannot walk can be carried; a Berner cannot. Your dog's breeder and your veterinarian may help you decide.

If you can, the kindest way is to stay with the dog when he is euthanized. He will lie on the floor with his head on your lap. An injection in his front leg will allow him to relax and go to sleep, at last being out of pain.

The other big decision is the final resting-place for your dog. You can bury your Berner, but he is a big dog so it will be a big task. Burying him on your property is viable for those who don't plan to move and if local ordinances allow. There are pet cemeteries available to consider as an alternate. Many people leave their dogs at the veterinarian, not knowing what happens to them. A mass grave or a landfill may be the final resting-place. Cremation is available through many veterinary practices for a fee. You may keep the cremains or bury them. If you are not sure, discuss with your veterinarian the best choice for you and your Bernese.

If possible, consider these choices well before the decisions need to be made. It is much harder to make such decisions when you are coping with illness and grief.

HOW-TO: MONITOR YOUR

Look at your dog every day. Examine him thoroughly during your grooming and brushing. Write down everything you notice and tell your veterinarian.

Input and Output

Are there any changes in his eating or drinking? Is he consuming more or less? Is he urinating more or less, or does he strain? Are there changes in his stool or the frequency of defecation? Is there any blood in his urine or stool? Is he vomiting? If so, what comes up?

Posture and Carriage

Notice any differences in his posture, movement, or activity. Has his energy level or mood altered? Does he limp; is he stiff or uncoordinated? Is he more irritable? More lethargic? Is his breathing labored? Does he stand with his head down and his back rounded? Does he only want to lie down or only want to stand?

Changes to His Body

When you brush or bathe your Berner, be aware of any lumps, bumps, or abrasions. With a breed that may have cancer, bumps need to be brought to the attention of your veterinarian. Run your hands over his whole body. Does it feel the same on both sides? Do you notice any changes in his bones? Is any area sensitive or tender? If your male is intact, confirm that his testicles feel the same and haven't changed in size. See if there is discharge from any orifice, including nose, mouth, vulva or penis, and anus.

Coat as a Health Barometer

Health problems often show up in your Berner's coat. Are there changes in his coat? Has the texture or quantity changed? Are there bare patches? Is the coat unusually oily or dry? Is he scratching regularly? Is he licking or chewing at a part of his body? He may have an allergy, mange, parasites, or other issues that your veterinarian can help you identify and correct.

Notice when your dog's posture and expression indicate that he doesn't feel well.

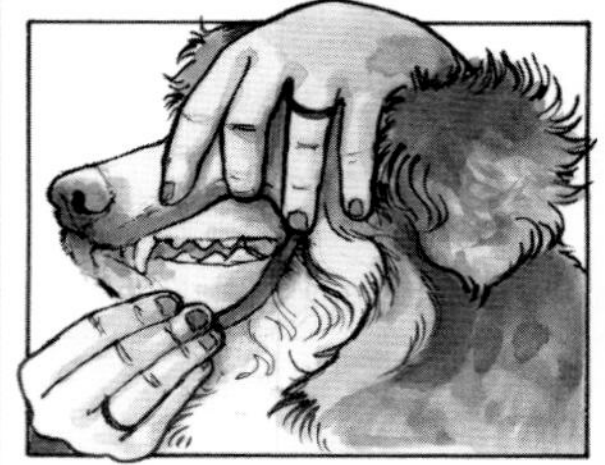

Examine your Berner's mouth and teeth as part of his regular at-home checkup.

Heads Up

Check his eyes. Are they unusually red? Are they tearing more than normal? Look in his mouth. His teeth should be strong, white, and clean. Be sure to brush them regularly. His gums may be pink or dark, depending on his pigment. Determine what is normal for your dog, so you will know if they are pale. Look in his ears for infections or parasites. If he is scratching around his head, there is usually a reason.

Taking Your Dog's Temperature

Take your dog's temperature if you suspect he might be sick. Normal canine temperature is between 101 and 102°F (38 and 39°C). If your dog's temperature is more than one degree higher or lower, call your veterinarian. If it is more than two degrees higher or lower, take your dog to a veterinarian immediately.

Giving Medication

Open your dog's mouth and place the pill as far back on his tongue as you can. Push it farther back with a finger, then hold his mouth closed so he will swallow. If you would rather not do this or if he objects strenuously, you can hide the pill in a piece of soft cheese, meat, or peanut butter.

Liquid medicine can be a challenge to dog owners. A syringe with the needle removed is a handy tool for this task. Draw the measured liquid into the syringe. Hold your dog's head slightly tilting upward. Put the syringe inside the dog's cheek and squirt the liquid as far back as you can comfortably get. The liquid will slip behind his teeth, and he should swallow it. Hold his mouth closed and tilted up until he swallows.

Doggy Medicine Chest

There are some nonprescription products that you can keep on hand for your Berner. Check with your veterinarian for guidance.

- Tape and sterile gauze bandages can be used in an emergency.
- Hydrogen peroxide can be used to clean a wound.
- In a pinch, unflavored gelatin can be used to stop bleeding.
- Antibiotic ointment, antidiarrhea medicine, eye ointment, baby aspirin, and upset stomach medication including a product with simethicone, can be included in a first aid kit.

Examine your whole dog weekly with your hands to determine if you can find any problems.

- Aspirin is effective with dogs, but Tylenol and ibuprofen are not.

Consult with your veterinarian first before medicating your Berner.

Sources for Health Information

While there is much misinformation on the Internet, there are a few sites that can provide additional information about health conditions that may affect your dog. The BMDCA site at *www.bmdca.org* has multiple pages dedicated to health issues. The OFA site at *www.offa.org* has extensive information about the conditions it evaluates. The Berner-Garde Foundation (BGF) was established to gather and provide information about genetic diseases affecting the Bernese Mountain Dog. You can access BGF at *www.bernergarde.org*, which is a link from the BMDCA Web site home page.

After Seeing Your Veterinarian

After visiting the veterinarian, follow the treatment and give the medicine according to her instructions. Closely watch your Berner to see if he is responding to the treatment and medication prescribed. If he isn't, tell your veterinarian and schedule another visit—don't just wait and hope the dog will get better.

FUN WITH YOUR BERNESE

Bernese Mountain Dogs were developed as all-around farm dogs, capable and willing to do many jobs. While few are farm hands today, they are willing and very able to do many jobs and to learn new tasks. You and your Berner can pursue many activities together.

Canine Good Citizen

AKC's Canine Good Citizens program recognizes dogs that are well-behaved at home and in the community. Dogs of any age, even puppies that have had their vaccinations, can be tested, certified, and earn the title CGC after their names.

Many obedience training clubs offer classes to prepare people for the CGC tests, following beginning and basic classes. Some offer the CGC tests at the conclusion of the class. If your Berner passes these tests, you can send the test results signed by the certified evaluator to AKC with a small fee to get your CGC certificate.

Your Berner is waiting—waiting for you to get off the couch, to come home from work, to make time for her, and to have some fun!

Obedience

If you and your Berner enjoyed training and she has earned her CGC title, you can investigate obedience titles. There are three levels offered by AKC. The first level, Novice, has your dog performing common behaviors wanted in a companion dog. In the Novice class at obedience trials, a dog can earn a Companion Dog or CD title. The higher levels are more challenging, but take advantage of many behaviors that dogs enjoy doing, such as retrieving, jumping, and finding things with their sense of smell. AKC obedience competition events are called obedience trials. Attend some in your area, and you'll get inspired to come home and train your dog.

Each level has a set of exercises that your Berner (and you) must do satisfactorily. You start with a total of 200 points, earned by doing individual exercises. Each time you or

Rally is an exciting, fast-moving companion event where you and your dog work as a team, having fun and earning titles.

your Berner don't do an exercise correctly, points are deducted. You must score at least half of the available points for each exercise, and you need at least 170 total points to pass. If you and your dog pass, you have earned a leg, and when you have three legs, your Berner has the title!

Companion Dog is the first level. The Novice exercises to earn the CD title are *heel* on lead and off lead, *figure eight, stand for exam, recall*, long *sit*, and long *down*. Most of the exercises are done with you and your Berner alone. But the long *sit* and long *down* are done with other dogs and their owners in the ring with you and your dog.

Companion Dog Excellent (CDX) is the next level after CD. The exercises in the Open class are all done off lead and include *heel free* and *figure eight, drop on recall, retrieve on flat, retrieve* over high jump, *broad jump*, long *sit*, and long *down*.

Utility (UD) is the highest level of AKC obedience. The Utility exercises include the hand signal exercises, directed retrieve, directed jumping, moving stand for examination, and scent discrimination.

Rally

Rally is AKC's latest competitive event that offers titles. It combines some of the obedience exercises with some of the speed and excitement of agility. Dogs can compete in Rally before, during, or after working on obedience titles. Each dog and handler go through a course set up by the judge with 10 to 20 stations. Each station instructs you and your dog to do something, such as *sit, down, turn*, and *call* your dog. You can talk to your dog, praise and encourage her, but you cannot touch her.

Rally has multiple levels of classes and titles that vary in the number of stations and the types of instructions specified at each station. Rally Novice is done with the dog on lead, but the advanced and excellent classes have the dog off lead. Higher-level classes include harder instructions or exercises, such as jumps, and have more stations. Titles available include Rally Novice, Rally Advanced, and Rally Excellent.

Agility

Agility started in England, and the AKC held its first agility trial in 1994. It has become the most popular, fastest-growing, and fastest-

TIP

CGC Exercises

The following are the tests your Berner needs to pass to earn her CGC.

- Accepting a friendly stranger who approaches you and your dog.
- Sitting politely by your side for petting by the friendly stranger.
- Appearance and grooming; permitting someone to examine and groom her.
- Walking on a loose lead.
- Walking through a crowd.
- *Sit* and *Down* on command and staying in place.
- Coming when called by you when she is about 10 feet (3 m) away.
- Reaction to another dog.
- Reaction to distraction showing that the dog doesn't startle excessively when inappropriate.
- Supervised separation.

Agility courses are created with obstacles the dog must perform correctly. Here, a Bernese Mountain Dog is seen going through a tire jump obstacle.

paced AKC companion event. At agility competitions, called trials, each dog with her handler runs through an obstacle course. The handler can talk to and encourage his dog, making it a fun and exciting event for both. If you and your Berner like training and are reasonably athletic, this could be an event for you.

Obstacles: The obstacles your dog will encounter in agility include the A-frame, several jumps, tunnels, weave poles, the dog walk, and a pause table. Your Berner runs up, over, and through the obstacles in sequence, taking her cues from you, racing the clock.

Levels: There are three levels of competition: Novice, Open, and Excellent. They vary with the number, types, and placement of obstacles on the course, the size of the course, and the amount of communication allowed between the dog and handler.

Standard courses include all the obstacles. A "jumpers with weaves" course includes only those obstacles that are not considered "contact" obstacles, where the dog must touch a specified part of the obstacle. "Preferred" classes have lower jump heights and longer standard times.

Even today, Berners can enjoy pulling carts. This can be a useful activity, as shown here, as this Berner pulls a cart full of firewood.

Each time your dog gets a qualifying score on a course, she gets a leg toward her title. It takes three legs to earn a title. Several agility titles are available, depending on the different combinations of level, type of course, and whether it is "preferred" or not. The height of the jumps will be adjusted based on the height of the dog, but the other obstacles don't change. This gives certain-sized fast and athletic dogs an advantage, and it is a challenge for especially small and large dogs. If it appeals to you, your Berner and you can try and may find that you enjoy agility.

Drafting

Bernese Mountain Dogs pulled carts in their Swiss ancestral home, so it is natural for Berner owners to be interested in this activity. The Bernese Mountain Dog Club of America and some affiliate clubs offer drafting events at which Berners can earn titles that recognize the dogs' abilities to do one of their original and important functions.

If you and your Berner want to pursue drafting or carting activities, remember to have fun and stay mindful of the comfort and safety of your dog. Your dog must be temperamentally, emotionally, and physically sound, and willing to get involved in drafting. She should be at least one year old or older before being asked to pull anything and physically mature before pulling any weight. In addition to earning titles, she may participate in local parades, take your young kids for a ride, or even haul things around your property.

Titles

The BMDCA offers several titles to encourage, develop, and demonstrate drafting ability in

TIP

Types of Equipment to Pull

✔ Cart—two-wheeled vehicle; easy and lightweight, but may tip if not properly loaded.

✔ Wagon—four-wheeled vehicle; larger, heavier, more stable.

✔ Travois—device used by native Americans for transporting goods; resembles a stretcher held at one end and dragged.

✔ Sled—has runners to slide across ice and snow.

✔ Toboggan—like a sled, but with no runners.

Note: Most sleds and toboggans have no brakes, so use with care so the device doesn't bump into the dog.

Berners. There is a Novice Draft Dog (NDD) title and a Draft Dog (DD) title that dogs can earn individually. The NDD exercises are performed on lead; the DD exercises are done off lead. Equivalent brace titles are available for a pair of dogs that work together.

Drafting events include the following exercises:

- Basic control, including *heel*, *down-stay*, and *recall*.
- Willingness to be harnessed and hitched.
- Control with distractions when hitched to a rig.
- Basic drafting commands such as *forward*, *stop*, and *back up*.
- Maneuvering turns and obstacles.
- Ability to haul a load for a distance, such as a half mile.

Other titles are available also through the parent club. The Working Dog Award is offered by BMDCA to Berners with a Novice DD title and any two of the following titles: obedience Companion Dog (CD), Tracking Dog (TD), Novice Agility (NA), and Junior Herding Dog (JHD). BMDCA offers the Versatility Award to Berners that are AKC champions, have the NDD title, and one of these titles: CD, TD, NA, and JHD.

Other organizations offer draft competitions and titles that Berners can participate in. Among these are the Greater Swiss Mountain Dog Club of America, the Newfoundland Club of America, the Great Pyrenees Club of America, and the Canadian Kennel Club.

Harnesses

The harness used for carting should be of good quality, one that doesn't rub or irritate your dog. There are two styles: Siwash and buckle. The Siwash style has a shoulder and neck harness that the dog pushes against. It is safer in that it allows free movement of the

This is an example of a Siwash-style harness.

Before having two Berners pull a cart together, make certain that each dog is skilled at carting alone and that the two dogs are friends.

dog's shoulders. The buckle harness has a cross-chest band that the dog pushes against.

Training

Before you begin carting, master basic obedience commands. Your dog should respond reliably to *Come*, *Sit*, *Down*, *Heel*, *Stand*, and *Stay*.

Accustom your dog to the harness before putting it on her. Let her sniff and investigate (but not chew) it. Progress to laying it on her back so she experiences the feel of it. When she is comfortable, let her wear it while doing her normal activities, but not pulling anything.

When she wears it without noticing it, attach some ropes so that she is dragging something around. Add some small objects to the ropes, so she feels some light weight to pull. Teach her some actual carting commands, so that she will start and stop on command, and turn right and left.

As with the harness, let her investigate the cart without being attached to it. Have it around for a few days so that she can check it out thoroughly. Move it around so that she can see that it moves.

Hitch her to the cart, letting her see what you are doing. Have someone else hold her collar and lead so that she doesn't run off with the cart attached and panic. Hitch and unhitch her multiple times over several days.

When you are ready for her to start pulling, you or a friend should walk with her, holding her collar. Let her learn by pulling an empty cart. Give her as much time as she needs; some dogs learn faster than others. Give her lots of praise and rewards for doing such a fine job.

This Berner waits patiently as she prepares to pull her cart in the upcoming parade.

Tracking

Bernese Mountain Dogs are not famous for using their noses to find things, but a dog's sense of smell is many times more powerful than a human's, so you can consider tracking as a fun event to try. AKC offers tracking competition and titles to recognize a dog's ability to follow a human scent. Unlike other AKC competitions, your dog needs to qualify only once to earn the title.

There are several levels of tracking titles. TD for Tracking Dog is the first. TDX, or Tracking Dog Excellent, has the dog following a longer, older track. Variable Surface Tracking (VST) has the dog following a track that crosses different surfaces, including possibly ground, pavement, and in a building.

Like all training, you use lots of treats and train in increments. Lay a short track, about 6 feet (2 m), in the grass, shuffling your feet as you do so. Put treats along the track and at the end. With your dog on lead, show her the beginning of the track and encourage her to follow the scent and find the treats. Enthusiastically praise her success. As she gets the concept, you can lengthen the track and even introduce a few turns.

Herding

Herding is a modification of a dog's basic hunting instinct. In their original jobs as all-round farm dogs, Bernese Mountain Dogs herded the farmer's few cattle to the pasture to graze and later back to the barn. Berners were considered drovers, working closely with mild-mannered, slow dairy cattle. They walk normally behind the cattle, not racing around, not crouching, not staring down the cows. Their style is quite different from Border Collies and many other herding dogs.

Note: If you want to try herding with your Berner, make sure you work with a trainer who understands the Berner's way of working.

Trials: While AKC has herding events, Bernese Mountain Dogs are not allowed to participate. However, Berners can participate in American Herding Breed Association (AHBA) tests and trials.

The AHBA offers two types of trial classes, Herding Trial Dog and Herding Ranch Dog, each with three levels. It also has a test program with two levels: the Herding Dog Capability Test (HCT) and the Junior Herding Dog Test (JHD). The HCT is a pass/fail test to identify herding instinct and the ability of the dog to move stock under the direction of the handler. The JHD requires that the dog have some training and has the dog move the stock around several obstacles and into a pen.

If you would like to try herding, find an experienced herding trainer to work with. He should be able to provide instruction as well as a place to work and stock to work with, likely sheep or possibly goats. Your dog's first experience with stock should be with stock that are accustomed to dogs, so that she has a good experience.

Before you try herding, make sure that your dog has a very solid off-lead recall and that she will reliably sit or lie down on command from a distance. You need to be able to control your dog around stock.

Therapy Dog

If you are interested and your Berner enjoys visiting with people, consider sharing her with people who love dogs, but who cannot have one anymore. You can participate in Therapy dogs.

Therapy dogs visit people in care facilities who don't have access to dogs. The dogs bring friendship and entertainment to those who enjoy canine company. It has been shown that visiting dogs reduce stress and can actually improve the health of those they visit.

Therapy dogs can visit schools, special education programs, nursing homes, assisted-living facilities, children's homes, and other places receptive to dogs. Dogs are used for children to read to, resulting in the children reading more and improving their skills.

There are national, regional, and local organizations that register Therapy dogs. They test the dogs to certify that they are suitable for Therapy dog visits, that they have good temperaments, are stable and accepting of medical and patient equipment, and are adequately trained to behave. You may visit a place alone with your Berner, or you can go as part of a group if there are other Therapy dogs in your area.

Show Dog

You have seen dog shows on television; perhaps the first Bernese Mountain Dog you saw was at a dog show. Maybe you'd like your beautiful dog out there competing, too. If she's as nice as you think, she may be able to earn the title of Champion.

Many Berners have been quite successful as therapy dogs and, to a limited extent, as search and rescue dogs.

If you would like to show your Berner, tell your breeder before you get a puppy that you would like a show-potential puppy. He'll help you select one that he believes will be competitive at dog shows. Dogs that compete at dog shows must be intact, so you cannot spay or neuter your dog. You'll need to train your dog to trot at your side in a straight line and to stand and let the judge examine her.

At dog shows, judges evaluate the dogs to see which ones they feel are the closest to the standard, the document that describes the perfect Berner. After examining all the dogs, the judge selects one male and one female to get points toward their championships. When a Berner has enough points, she will be a Champion.

While dog shows on television look very elaborate, there are many shows around the country that are much more down to earth, where people like you show their own dogs and win. It is a great family sport, fun for you and your dog, and an opportunity to meet other Berner owners.

HOW-TO: FIND DOG

The Internet is an excellent tool to find events and activities that you can enjoy with your dog. The American Kennel Club and its local clubs sponsor the most events. The BMDCA and its affiliate clubs put on many events around the country, too, especially for Berners.

American Kennel Club

AKC's official Web site is *www.akc.org*. Click on *Events* to navigate to a page that lists the types of events that AKC sponsors. Some are restricted to specific dogs, while other events are open to all AKC-recognized purebred dogs.

From the *Events* page, you can click on each type of activity you are interested in in order to learn more about it. The activities that are available to most purebred dogs are:

- Agility
- Canine Good Citizen
- Conformation Dog Shows
- Obedience
- Rally
- Tracking

Explore some of the Bernese Mountain Dog's world on the Internet.

Events and Awards

To find scheduled events in your area, click on *Events and Awards Search*. From that page, with the tab on *Event Search*, you can find events that are not breed-specific. Select the state you want searched; you can specify more than one. Pick the time period you are interested in. "From Today Forward" will get you all future events that sponsoring clubs have applied to hold. Choose the type of event you are looking for, then click *Search*.

The events matching your criteria will be displayed in chronological order. The list will include the club giving the event, the city where it will be held, the type of event, and the date of the event. Under the club name is a link to more club information.

Conformation

On the *Events and Awards Search* page, if you select the *Conformation* tab, you get a slightly different search page—one where you can specify the breed for which you want dog show information. Again, select the state or states and the time period for which you want events. A list of events will be displayed, with the name of the club, the location and date, the show secretary/superintendent, and the judges for the selected breed.

Obedience

From the *Events and Awards Search* page, you can also search for obedience, rally, and agility events. Note that some clubs sponsor events that combine more than one type of activity, such as a dog show, obedience trial, and rally.

Some Canine Good Citizen classes and tests can be located by selecting *Training/Testing* from the *Canine Good Citizens* page. Many obedience clubs offer classes without listing them with AKC, so you can contact your nearest obedience club to see what classes they recommend for CGC and when they schedule CGC testing.

Local Clubs

Events and classes are usually put on by clubs. From AKC's home page, click the *Clubs* navigation button. From the *Clubs* page, click *Club Search* to find clubs in your area. First select the type of club you want to find: agility, conformation (dog show), or obedience, among others. From the selected page, choose the state, and *Search*. On the *Conformation* page, you can also specify a breed if you want to find a specialty or one-breed-only club.

Most clubs sponsor events, and many offer training classes. The club contact can give you information about both. Some clubs have informed AKC that they are holding training classes. If you select *Training Clubs* on the *Club Search* page, you will get a list of these clubs. Many clubs offer classes, but are not listed on the *Training Clubs* page. Contact your area clubs to learn more.

Bernese Mountain Dog Club of America

The BMDCA and its affiliate clubs put on many events especially for Berners. Some events are titling ones, where dogs can earn championships or drafting titles. Others are more informal, such as meetings, matches, and get-togethers with other Berner owners.

One event you want to consider attending is the national specialty. It is a week-long celebration of Bernese Mountain Dogs. It includes a regular dog show plus a futurity, which is a special competition for the younger dogs. It also includes drafting, herding, obedience, tracking, rally, and agility events, and the opportunity to get to know Berner fans and their dogs from all over the country. From the BMDCA Web site home page, click on the link for the *Specialty* for the current year for information for the next national specialty.

The BMDCA home page also has a link for *Events* that will take you to a calendar of events scheduled for Berners across the country. Clicking on the event name will get you information about that event.

If you have the resources and inclination, you and your Berner can experience and enjoy her original function of carting.

Drafting

If you are interested in drafting, highlight the *Drafting* button on the home page and select the *Draft Calendar*. You will see a list of scheduled drafting tests. Click on one to find more information about it, including a contact person.

Affiliate Clubs

Affiliate clubs are local or regional Bernese Mountain Dog clubs whose members own that breed. They meet regularly, put on events, and other activities. These club activities are good places to meet other Berner owners and to learn more about the breed. Under *Breed Clubs* on the BMDCA Web site is a list of affiliate clubs.

The American Herding Breed Association

If you might be interested in herding with your Berner or would just like to see what dogs herding stock involves, access the AHBA Web site at *www.ahba-herding.org*. The menu and links are at the bottom of the page. Click on *Upcoming AHBA Trials* to get a list of scheduled events.

INFORMATION

Organizations

Note: Officers and contacts will change. Web sites should contain current information.

American Herding Breed Association
www.ahba-herding.org
Sharon Anderson, President
tervherd@ahba-herding.org

American Kennel Club
580 Centerview Drive
Raleigh, NC 27606-3390
(919) 233-9767
www.akc.org

Bernese Mountain Dog Club of America
Anne Copeland, Corresponding Secretary
PO Box 2675
Palatine, IL 60078-2675
www.bmdca.org
annes4@aol.com

Canadian Kennel Club
89 Skyway Avenue, Suite 100
Etobicoke, Ontario
M9W 6R4
(416) 675-5511
www.ckc.ca

The Kennel Club
1-5 Clarges Street
Piccadilly, London W1J 8AB
www.thekennelclub.org.uk

Magazines

AKC Gazette
General dog and multibreed magazine.
Contact AKC for subscription information.

THE ALPENHORN
Official bimonthly publication of the BMDCA
Roxanne Bortnick, subscriptions
1922 Cherry Lane
Johnstown, CO 80534
Bernese@warpdriveonline.com

Books

Donaldson, Jean. *Culture Clash*. Berkley, CA: James & Kenneth Publishers, 1997.

Guenter, Bernd. *The Bernese Mountain Dog: A Dog of Destiny.* Phoenix, AZ: Doral Publishing Co., 2004.

Ostermiller, Lilian. *Bernese Mountain Dogs.* Neptune City, NJ: T.F.H., 1993.

Russ, Diane and Shirle Rogers. *The Beautiful Bernese Mountain Dogs.* Loveland, CO: Alpine Publications, 1993.

Simonds, Jude. *The Complete Bernese Mountain Dog.* New York, NY: Howell Book House, 1989.

Smith, Sharon Chestnut. *The New Bernese Mountain Dog.* New York, NY: Howell Book House, 1995.

Willis, Dr. Malcolm B. *The Bernese Mountain Dog Today.* New York, NY: Howell Book House, 1998.

Even a cute puppy can have a bad hair day.

INDEX

About the Author

Nikki Riggsbee is an award-winning author of multiple articles and books directed at both pet owners and the dog showing public. She has shown and bred dogs for over twenty-five years, and judges more than sixty breeds at AKC dog shows. As a breeder, she guides prospective owners in their selection and educates them on how to best care for that specific breed. Nikki believes getting a dog is like adding a member to the family—it should be a life-long commitment.

Acknowledgments

The author is sincerely grateful to the Bernese Mountain Dog owners and breeders who shared their dogs and their knowledge for the benefit of this book. A special thank you goes to Mary Ellen Guy for her invaluable feedback and expertise. Appreciation to the folks at Barron's who offered suggestions and fine-tuning, especially to editor Anne McNamara, for all her help, patience, and good humor.

Important Note

This pet owner's manual tells the reader how to buy or adopt and care for a Bernese Mountain Dog. The author and publisher consider it important to point out that the advice given in the book is meant primarily for normally developed dogs of excellent physical health and sound temperament.

Anyone who acquires a fully-grown dog should be aware that the animal has already formed its basic impressions of human beings. The new owner should observe the animal carefully, including its behavior toward humans, and, whenever possible, should meet the previous owner.

Caution is further advised in the association of children with dogs, in meeting with other dogs, and in exercising the dog without a leash.

Even well-behaved and carefully supervised dogs can sometimes damage property or cause accidents. It is therefore in the owner's interest to be adequately insured against such eventualities, and we strongly urge all dog owners to purchase a liability policy that also covers their dog.

Photo Credits

Kent Akselsen: 11, 29, 30, 31, 39, 40, 45 (top and bottom), 46, 47, 48, 49, 50, 51 (top), 54, 55, 56, 60, 64, 69, 72, and 74; Norvia Behling: 13, 32, 35, 41, 42, and 51 (bottom); Kent Dannen: 4, 9, 36, 57, 73, 76, 81, 84, 86, and 87; Tara Darling: 2–3, 14, 23, 33, 61, 62, 66, 70, and 89; Cheryl Ertelt: 5, 16, 18, 19, 22, 24, 25, 27, 34, 43, 53, and 63; Isabelle Francais: 6, 8, 20, 28, 52, 68, 80, 82, 83, and 93; Karen Hudson: 17; Pets by Paulette: 59.

Cover Photos

Tara Darling: front cover and inside front cover; Pets by Paulette: back cover; Kent Dannen: inside back cover.

All inquiries should be addressed to:
Barron's Educational Series, Inc.
250 Wireless Boulevard
Hauppauge, NY 11788
www.barronseduc.com

ISBN-13: 978-0-7641-3592-7
ISBN-10: 0-7641-3592-9

Library of Congress Catalog Card No. 2006034342

Library of Congress Cataloging-in-Publication Data
Riggsbee, Nikki.
Bernese mountain dogs : everything about history, purchase, care, nutrition, training, and behavior / Nikki Riggsbee ; illustrations by Michele Earle-Bridges.
p. cm. — (A complete pet owner's manual)
Includes index.
ISBN-13: 978-0-7641-3592-7
ISBN-10: 0-7641-3592-9
1. Bernese mountain dog. I. Earle-Bridges, Michele. II. Title.

SF429.B47R54 2007
636.73—dc22 2006034342

Printed in China
9 8 7 6 5 4 3 2 1